BLAME THOU NOT HIM WHO DARES

A Fictional Autobiography of
Matthew Arnold
In Which He Saves a Girl's Life and . .
.

By Matthew Arnold

(Ghostwritten by
Marguerite McKeon)

By John K. Press, Ph.D.

Social Books
Seoul, Korea

© Social Books 2016
pressjohn@hotmail.com

Work authored by John Kenneth Press, Ph.D.

All rights reserved. No part of this publication may be reproduced, stored in a retrieval system or transmitted, in any form, or by any means, electronic, mechanical, recorded, photocopied, or otherwise, without the prior permission of the copyright owner, except by a reviewer who may quote brief passages in a review.

Library of Congress Subject Headings:
Biography, History, Young Adult Fiction, Victorian Studies, Matthew Arnold, Culturist, Culturism, Poetry, Literary Criticism, multicultural

ISBN: 97809785777-8-0

Printed in the United States of America

Matthew Arnold resources may be found at www.matthewarnold.us

Culturism resources may be found at www.culturism.us

Cover and interior layout design by Divine Tree www.vedicdesign.com

BLAME THOU NOT HIM WHO DARES

A Fictional Autobiography of
Matthew Arnold
In Which He Saves a Girl's Life and . .
.

By Matthew Arnold

(Ghostwritten by
Marguerite McKeon)

By John K. Press, Ph.D.

Dedicated to Lawrence Peter Levine,
whose love, writing and life continue to inspire us.

Blame thou not, therefore, him who dares
Judge vain beforehand human cares;
Whose natural insight can discern
What through experience others learn;
Who needs not love and power, to know
Love transient, power an unreal show;
Who treads at ease life's uncheer'd ways;
Him blame not, Fausta, rather praise.

-Matthew Arnold (1822 – 1888)
From the poem, Resignation

Table of Contents

BACK FROM THE DEAD 1
MARGUERITE'S BIOGRAPHY 8
MARGUERITE'S FRIENDS 14
CHILDHOOD AND INNOCENCE 19
SUICIDE 24
DARKNESS AND LIGHT 29
POETRY 39
ARNOLD GOES TO SCHOOL 53
MARGUERITE'S PLAN 65
FAMILY DYNAMICS 73
EDUCATION 80
ROAD TRIP 97
PAST, PRESENT, FUTURE 105
CRITICISM 117
HOMESICKNESS 132
CULTURE AND ANARCHY 150
LIFE AND DEATH 161
THE CHURCH OF ARNOLD 173
FAILURE 188
HOME AGAIN 198
EPILOGUE 205

CHAPTER

~ 1 ~

BACK FROM THE DEAD

What a life young Marguerite Buckby had lived. Three months into her seventeenth year, she had lived in three cities and lost two mothers. Her birth mother gave her up for adoption; her adopted mother left the family when Marguerite was scarcely eight.

I do not know why the powers decided that sending *me* back to save *her* life had a chance. I lived from 1822 to 1888: The Victorian Era. But, my last assignment was in the early 1960s. I still resonated with people then. And, even then, I was rarely sent to people younger than thirty years of age. I seem an odd fit for a jaded teenage girl bent on suicide in this age. Why her? Why now?

Another question I have is, "Why am I here?" I mean, not just here with Marguerite, but here at all. Usually, very quickly after having had a helpful interaction with the person to whom I am assigned, after saving their life or helping them make the right decision, I quickly fade away; I return to the netherworld. But, as I write this, Marguerite seems out of danger. And yet, I am still here.

Wonderfully, for the first time in my hundred-plus years of guiding, my extended time with Marguerite has afforded me some time to write. Since I am her guide, I am writing about young Marguerite. And, as I might disappear at any time, I'll quickly hasten back to her narrative. But, I wanted to share my puzzlement and joy over my ability to write these very words.

While alive, my day job, as it were, was working as a school inspector. I would get on trains and travel from county to county, across much of England, inspecting schools. As such, it seems appropriate that my first contact with Marguerite happened in her school's library.

We never know what large results might bloom from small gestures. Mr. Early asked the students in his English Literature course to write a paper on the life of a poet from their literature anthology book. It just so happened that, although over one hundred years separated us, my poem *Dover Beach* spoke to young Marguerite. Though I don't know why I'm here for her, that poem brought me to her attention.

At Dover beach I stood and contemplated lost love, life, and time. The waves moving in and out seemed to wash away all of my previous burning longings, to render them silent – to bring me a sad peace. Marguerite could relate to my mournful state.

While Marguerite enjoyed the poem and the encyclopedia entry about me, her attention barely wavered from her own emotional state. My young charge could only remember a few distant good times. And, she doubted she'd ever feel happiness again.

Her young mind attributed her emotional state to events in her own life rather than looking for the source of her malady in social forces. Why had her birth mother thrown her away? Why had her adopted mother refused her phone calls for so long? Would she ever have a normal conversation or connection with her father? And, somewhere in this mix, her boyfriend, Ricky, tormented her thoughts.

"Marguerite!" The second encyclopedia column conveyed that, "Arnold loved a mysterious woman named Marguerite." Yes. I wrote a few poems about my love for this young lady. This coincidence of names provided some justification for my having been sent to guide Marguerite. But, it seemed too incidental to fully account for their having assigned her to me - let alone my being able to stay with her for extended amount of time.

When Marguerite read about my Marguerite, she had an epiphany; "Marguerites had loved and lost before." This led to the realization that people in the past actually existed, were flesh and blood persons. Others had actually been Marguerite too. Joy filled my earth-bound soul. Such epiphanies are priceless. Oh, by the way, we guides can often hear our charges' thoughts.

Marguerite eagerly read on, "Arnold met Marguerite while on holiday in Switzerland. She inspired some of his strongest poems. Although Arnold visited the hotel in which she worked for two consecutive years, scholars have never been able to determine Marguerite's identity or if she actually existed." Marguerite intuitively knew and said to herself, "No, Marguerite was real, as real as I am."

As she read these words, I felt my blood boil. "Philistines!" I shrieked, "Rather than grovel after sordid trysts, you should pursue perfection, improve your nation."

Marguerite turned abruptly in my direction, "Who's there?" she demanded aloud. A nosey (and terribly frumpy) girl looked around the end of the bookshelves. Marguerite was embarrassed at having been seen speaking to no one. But, though she saw nothing, Marguerite had definitely felt my presence. As the past was becoming real to her, I was becoming real to her.

Marguerite gave the girl a wave of the hand, but not the satisfaction of eye contact. Marguerite sank back into wondering about the Marguerite before her. And, only a few minutes later did she register the disappearance of the usual predominance of gossip in her head. At that, my new friend and charge smiled. She had disappeared into a question about the past and it had erased the petty nuisance of those around her. She savored this moment.

After all, Marguerite mused, the girl who responded to her question did not wish to rescue her from an assailant. No, her all-too-familiar salacious grin wet at the prospect of gossip. The girl's fondest wish had been to find her fighting with a boy, kissing a girl, or engaged in some other form of scandalous behavior so that she could proudly share gossip. Marguerite was positively ill with such lewdness. And, she savored her newfound ability to make others disappear by thinking about history.

Marguerite also tasted some of the same infatuation I had long ago felt towards my muse, the object of my first love, the Swiss Marguerite. She wondered about the palpable passion I had felt for this beautiful young spirit and what drove us apart.

What's more, my objections not registered, Marguerite felt awe over the romantic academic souls who had probably spent years of their lives trying to uncover the identity of a dead poet's early girlfriend. "Could such people really exist?"

And, for just a fleeting moment, young Marguerite Buckby had the scholarship bug. She had a puzzle that mattered more to her than constantly fighting with her stupid boyfriend and her lascivious, leering fellow students.

She wanted nothing more than to find out about this distant failed lover, me, Matthew Arnold, and his mystery love. There was no way for her to have known the fantastic fact that I too had been assigned to learn more about her.

I am one of a small cadre of angels who occasionally get to return to the land of the living and provide guidance to both troubled souls and people with vital questions. A step above guardian angels, we actually interact with humans in their times of need. Unimaginatively, as journalists might, we call ourselves 'guides.'

In heaven, (as you may call it), I can read and hear whatever people write about me. But, my understanding is faint, as if I were remembering reading something rather than actually reading it.

As glad as I am to have an afterlife, sometimes, having your existence prolonged and being able to hear people talk about you, in a half-awake state, and to know you're only half-awake and actually dead, is horrific. Still, it seems fair to me that as long as your work lingers in the fog of collective learning, a part of you lingers there too.

When back on earth, as now, my mind is crisp. To be alive again, or at least to be back on earth for a period of time, is exhilarating beyond belief. The smells and sights, and the edges of my own thoughts, are full and sharp again.

Dear Reader, you should always appreciate having a crisp mind and being in real situations. It is to Marguerite that I owe *my* gratitude for this return to earth. Without her researching me, I would not be having this very wonderful moment.

Though I died well over one hundred years ago, I still look as I did in my early forties. I believe I have returned at this age because I consider it my prime. At this age, I was a well-known critic and artist, and struck a rather dandified pose in the public mind. As photos of me from that age display, I sported wide mutton-chop sideburns and parted my hair in the middle.

At 6'2" I even lorded over large Americans. But any magnetism I might have exuded came not from my physical gifts, but my detailed ornamentation of those gifts. If you look closely at the photos, you'll see I wore – especially early on - the finest clothes. Sometimes I dressed to shock. I always cut quite the stylish figure!

My attention to ornamentation applied to my mental life as well. We all should, as I famously quipped, undertake a 'disinterested endeavor to learn and propagate the best that is known and thought in the world.' And I called the great middle class, who failed to care about anything but paychecks and gadgets, 'Philistines.'

Unfortunately, then as now, my daring to advocate standards, to denounce mediocrity, resulted in my having many intellectual enemies.

Happily, I made enough of an impression by teaching about beauty in this ugly world, that a number of scholars still study me. And, this continued attention has led to my preservation in the netherworld. And I suppose I will remain here, off and on, as long as a single soul is still thinking about me.

Normally the time on earth we are granted in our afterlife is very fleeting. I cannot believe that I have now been continually conscious for over an hour! Given time, I will chronicle all my adventures, with Marguerite, amongst the living. But first, I feel I must write a note to 'the-powers-that-be,' (or to the 'great not-ourselves,' as I used to call them).

Dearest Powers-that-be, I hope my chronicling this episode of guidance does not violate the terms of my heavenly parole. I suspect that your insight would lead you to guess that, as a writer, given extended time, I'd write.

If you wish me to stop writing, you can – of course - rip the pen and paper from my hand, and return me to the mist. But please know that writing gives me great joy and can only make me a better guide for young Marguerite. I very much appreciate both the time to write and the permission to do so.

Thank you Darlings!

CHAPTER
~ 2 ~

MARGUERITE'S BIOGRAPHY

As Dear Marguerite sat pondering the reality of my existence via the encyclopedia, she would have been shocked to know that she had her own encyclopedia entry, in a manner. You see, as a matter of course, we guides are given reports containing background information on our charges.

I found the description of her life at least as remote and strange as she must have found mine. The world has become tragic and unsafe for the young.

At the moment of her birth, in the Cleveland Clinic, in the American state of Ohio, her biological mother had already signed the adoption papers. As I read this, tears welled in my eyes.

In life, people thought my poetry's profundity had an air of contrivance, some claimed that I faked my emotions. Even my dear family expressed disbelief that their flippant son felt such melancholy. But, I felt the pathos of the world deeply.

To make matters worse, in the afterlife, my sense that people suffocate under a vale of tears – that they do not even dimly understand the miraculous nature of the very fact of their living – has greatly increased. I often wish to cry over peoples' blindness to the beauty of life.

As per the rules, we guides know no more about our charges than they know about themselves. And we must be aware that this self-knowledge can be a little treacherous; it oft rests upon half-truths and well-rehearsed defensive lies we tell ourselves to make ourselves right and maintain the uncomfortable reality to which we have become accustomed.

Marguerite, like others I have seen, takes this world seriously. But, more than others, I sense that she has a sense of detachment from her world. She cares about the little narratives that frame her life story, but not that much. This is both a strength and a danger.

Taking care of people in trouble - convincing them that life's spiritual jewels justify the tremendous efforts which continuing to live requires - tests ones' own faith. Believe me, I have immediate empathy for the pain Marguerite's stories bring her.

The ability to feel is so rich. But, it overwhelms me. It makes me forget, however momentarily, that I really am a happy fellow. And, I must remember my glee, and fight for emotional distance, to be a good guide.

Because I do not know more about the subjects than they know of themselves, I do not yet know much of anything about Marguerite's biological mother. She, however, looms large in this adopted orphan's mind. Marguerite feels that she cannot fully know herself until she meets this mother.

I was not adopted. I came from a large and stable family. As such, I cannot fully comprehend her need to meet her birth mother. Still, I hope that she someday fills this cavity and can stop dwelling on it.

Honestly, though, I think she would be better off getting to understand herself without reference to those who happen to be in her particular family line. Socrates is her sibling in the western family. She should get to know him. It would be healthier than brooding over a nearly random stranger.

Furthermore, I suspect that meeting the stranger who occasioned her birth will only add to Marguerite's sense of disappoint with this world.

I will not argue that we don't have innate dispositions that can become starker when face-to-face with our biological progenitors. Lord knows, I am very much like my father. But, our self-cultivation is what makes us worthwhile. And, in this regard, the average person is as much an orphan as my forlorn Marguerite.

In her eighth year, Marguerite's father, Jack Buckby, lost his job in a Cleveland factory. This happened so long ago that Marguerite does not remember the name of the factory. So the factory name, as other details I have searched for, Dear Reader, I cannot convey to you.

As her father's finances took a turn for the worse, the fidelity of Marguerite's adopted mother, Cynthia Rose Buckby, also declined. She took to spending more and more of her time with someone who could afford her drinking and increasing drug use; a man who – conveniently enough - sold drugs and enjoyed drink: Dr. Les Daniel Christianson.

When I later inquired as to what sort of doctor Dr. Les might have been, she replied, "I dunno. I was too young. Maybe medicine? I can't remember." Enigmatic.

When Cynthia made official her relocation to Dr. Christianson's apartment, Jack decided to relocate to Detroit. His parents, Bill and Charlotte Buckby, had a spare bedroom for their granddaughter and a couch for their son. And, Bill, some kind of low-level manager at a Chrysler automotive plant, got Jack full-time employment.

Unfortunately, corporate disengagement from the city that had birthed the automotive industry and a lack of fealty to the western world, meant more and more of the automotive jobs were sent to other nations. Seeing 'the writing on the wall,' as the Bible's Book of Daniel says, Jack accepted a friend's offer of employment in Los Angeles.

Jack did not only base his decision to relocate on his potential for employment. Cindy Rose, as he called his soon-to-be-ex wife, had gone from bad to worse. Marguerite's adopted mother made seeing her child less and less of a priority. And several times Jack had to cancel visits because, even over the phone, he could tell that she was heavily intoxicated.

Jack thought moving Marguerite to Los Angeles would provide a reasonable excuse to not see Cindy Rose and spare his daughter the pain of watching the only mother she had known destroy herself. Maggie, as Jack called his young Marguerite, would cry every time a date with Cindy Rose was cancelled. Moving to Los Angeles seemed like the safe and healthy thing to do.

Marguerite only half-believed her father's self-serving story of moving to protect her from abandonment. She sometimes accuses her father of stealing her away from her mother just for the promise of a more glamorous life in Los Angeles. As I have not met Jack Buckby, I have no intuition as to whether or not this accusation contains some truth.

Marguerite burns at never again having seen her now deceased grandparents. Jack had the money, but, as a person who never seemed to stop working, never had the time to visit them. She understands when her father tells her that he could not continue to live on his parents' couch forever. But, Marguerite, resents her father for not visiting the region after moving to Los Angeles.

At any rate, Jack Buckby's move turned out to be good for him. After an apprenticeship as a stagehand of sorts, under his friend's tutelage, he climbed to great success in the television industry. He employed a new-in-town, aw shucks, small town, I-am-no-threat-to-you routine to elicit training and introductions. In only seven years in Los Angeles he has worked on numerous shows, and now serves as the assistant-producer of the nationally popular situation comedy, 'Ted's Home.'

And, so from the outside, Marguerite's story has a happy ending. After being given away at birth and abandoned by her adopted mother, she has ended up the daughter of a successful television producer, with a nice home in the Hollywood Hills. She goes to a high school with lots of other children whose parents 'work in the industry.' As such, she is slated to enter this world of money and glamour.

Alas, Marguerite is depressed to the point of wanting to die. She, in fact, thinks about it daily. Some children quickly and easily manage the pain of their early abandonment. But Marguerite had bitterness deep in her muscles that she wore close to her skin. Her vulnerability corroded her sense of self.

And, Marguerite did not yet trust her father's new girlfriend, Samantha. In fact 'Scamantha's' very presence reminded her of the transitory nature of relationships – the meaninglessness of life. Even her 'late at the office again' father made her feel she was totally on her own.

CHAPTER

~ 3 ~

MARGUERITE'S FRIENDS

If you'll forgive the worn metaphysical language, Marguerite seems to have 'an old soul.' The very fact that she researched me in an encyclopedia's printed page, as opposed to doing so on the electric internet, testifies to her inchoate taste for the profound. For real pages have a pace and length, a breath – if you will - that penetrates the soul more deeply than the glowing screen does. She finds comfort in the touch, smell and sounds that pages offer.

Neither her interior nor the appearance of the taciturn youth had been communicated in the report on her. A slow developing girl, her 5' 6" body gives the appearance of a stick figure under a long stringy reddish dirty blonde mop. Her bones seem to float under her jeans and the long sleeved t-shirts she wears. Her small breasts, hidden in a slight bra, barely ever impact these shirts.

This last sartorial detail contains clues to her character. Her long sleeve t-shirts hide her gender. This reflects her reserved engagement with the salacious and trashy world. It reflects her all-important critical distance. She resides behind sunken eyes at times, as if recoiling from a bright light, a little terrified and insecure, within.

I relate to Marguerite's need to hide herself away. In my youth, I hid myself away in order to protect my poetic edge from the boring and mundane world.

Rather than depression, however, I found my powers best safeguarded behind outlandish clothes and hair that was "guiltless of English scissors." I also kept peoples' petty concerns at bay with a great sense of humor and a cutting ready wit. But, time permitting, more wonderful descriptions of me will follow later on.

Even at her happiest, Marguerite is naturally shy. And, though she speaks infrequently, her smirks provide loud commentary. The slight volume of her verbal output in no way implies a lack of opinions. She has great a capacity to see people's foolishness. Yet, as an old soul, she also has the capacity to find peoples' foolishness endearing. This probably explains her indulgence of people who are – to put it bluntly – trash.

A case in point is her boyfriend, Ricky. She is only with him because it stops gossip. People leave her alone when she posts, "I'm spending time with the BF today" on facebook. She even posts this when she has no plans to meet him.

Ricky is not only stupid – this is forgivable – he is disgusting. They share no interests and his very way of speaking, his slang, makes her skin crawl. But, he has so small a presence in her life that she can usually ignore him without too much friction. He provides more protection than annoyance.

If you couldn't tell, I despise Ricky. And it isn't just him as an individual; I loathe him as a type; as a generational type. This wretched rot has been pressuring Marguerite for more intimate relations for months. In monitoring her memories, I have heard him denigrate her. I will never understand the modern mentality by which young ladies get called "stupid," and "not that good looking," and stay with the swine who makes such less-than-chivalrous, unforgivably wounding remarks.

Alas, this is not particularly Marguerite or Ricky's fault – they are just examples of western culture's general abandonment of standards and values.

As evidence, I offer the fact that all of Marguerite's friends are brutal, shallow, philistines. Worse than philistines, they are vicious, ignorant, and proud. They remind me of what Hannah Arendt termed "the banality of fascism." Arendt, the story goes, sat across from some Nazis on a train. Rather than evil, crazy, or obsessed with a perverted ideal, (characteristics that would have *some* nobility), the soldiers were just stupid, empty, banal.

Marguerite's "best" friend, Philina, relentlessly tells Marguerite about the guys she's been speaking with on facebook; people my young charge has never met and has no interest in meeting. The on-line boys solicit intimacy from this young girl in the crudest ways and then call her "stuck up" and a "bitch" when she doesn't "put out." But these were the men that Philina sought out and sometimes even went out with.

Here is a sample of the horrid posts. Philina wrote, "I ain't hookin up wit U cuz U a cheep ass. I ain't comin to

U hous without U gittin me a taxi or some shit." The misspellings were not intentional. The reply, "U stuk up bitch. You betta git here so I kin tap that. I'll pay for U cab - one way. Bus back. I got some. I promises U a goot time."

These conversations sadden me. The human race has devolved to the point wherein it has no intelligence to uplift; no sense of beauty or the profound left, such as an awe of death might bring. And, as she is a sensitive being, I understand that Marguerite also feels her soul diminished and tainted by hearing such horrid banality passing for love, relationships or even conversation.

Marguerite cultivated the same sort of relationship with Philina that she had with her Ricky; she pretended to listen, while secretly wishing her friend would die. But, "Ya'gotta have friends." Besides, Philina had chosen Marguerite. But, my charge often wishes to slap Philina in the face and ask her "What the fuck are you talking about?" or "Who are you?" I like this instinct in her.

My darling charge also protects her soul from this nasty world via frequent retreats into the library. Her retreats gave me some hope for civilization.

Men, - if you'll permit some honest guidance, - you get easily ensnared by the unbelievable crudity of the modern age. If you have a hope of salvation, it lays most directly in your sense of honor. For men will fight violently for a cause. These days, the masculine sex wastes their umbrage on perceived personal slights and video games. But these energies could be bent towards more valiant ends if leadership would only provide pro-social mottos and causes.

And many women, despite the current encouragement to tart propensities, still retain a sense of the interior. When given a quiet space, they open a book and search with sincere interest. Some men would. But, given the action-sports mores, most males would be embarrassed to be found sitting at books undertaking prolonged inquiries nto the nature of their own souls.

The requirements of life and the grating pounding of her friends' needs, relentlessly scrapes at Marguerite's patience. While potentially a fun person, the sadness of her malaise overwhelms her soul. In a sort of nervous shock, she silently prays for all the sounds to stop.

And, yet, when she goes home, exactly the wrong sort of silence dominates – all is chipper and the past cannot be discussed. The new woman auditioning for the part of stepmother, Samantha, plays this game too well.

I write these words, having just finished observing another session of her researching me in the library. Beyond what may be wise, I am already feeling dangerously emotionally invested in my mission of preventing her from taking her own life.

I hope my levity will suffice to lift her spirits. The fact that I'm allowed to linger and write about this case makes me think my success is preordained. But, I don't know this to a certainty.

CHAPTER
~ 4 ~

CHILDHOOD AND INNOCENCE

In the weeks after I met her, Marguerite retreated further and further away from the world. She had found a place of solace to which to run: my childhood. She became obsessed with it. Its charm reassured her by half-way making her believe that goodness without cynicism could actually exist. Real or not, the very possibility of innocence comforted her. More immediately, preparing for her report gave her a reason to take a break from her world.

As the encyclopedia told Marguerite, my life had been a near total contrast to hers. I was born on December 24th, 1822. She pondered briefly the advantages and disadvantages of having one's birthday the day before Christmas before coming to the logical and true conclusion that, as she put it, "it musta sucked."

My father, Thomas Arnold, was the Head Master (Principal, in your words) of the famous Rugby high school. And, while tough and demanding, the boys all knew he loved them. He expected his young charges to be manly in living up to Christian precepts and morality – his technique got labeled 'muscular Christianity.' The young chaffed at the idea of disappointing him and worked to earn his approval. Of course, when others went home from school, and left Thomas Arnold's all-seeing eye, I did not.

Father loved to play with us. As I do, he had a very immature side. But, he was also a moralizing pedant. At the age of five, father started teaching each of his children Latin grammar, French verbs and exercises, arithmetic, history, geography and scripture. We memorized a hymn and short passage from the Bible every day for our father. When we turned six years old, Greek, German, and Italian were added.

"Can you imagine?" Marguerite thought, jealous of my education.

Wanting more detail than the encyclopedia offered, Marguerite checked out a copy of Nicholas Murray's 1996 biography of me, *A Life of Matthew Arnold*. In the afterlife, as I mentioned earlier, we get to read, see, and feel every mention of us by the living. As such, I am grateful to Dr. Murray. But, the title of his biography, always struck me as indicative of his not having reached any conclusions. What on earth does the awkward title, *A Life of Matthew Arnold*, convey?

At times, I even wondered if the title, *A Life of Matthew Arnold*, hints at my afterlife. Did he mean to indicate that I had more than one life? Since he could not possibly know about this, I have concluded that the title does not refer to my afterlife. It is just an unfortunate title that typifies the entire book's approach of simply chronicling one damn thing after another.

As an artist and social critic, I believe that all writing, history included, should have a point that ennobles mankind. Murray's book doesn't even have a point.

Marguerite eagerly consumed Murray's day-by-day description of my childhood and loved it. She enjoyed reading about my father's warmth. He had, for example, nicknames for all of his eight children. He dubbed me 'Crabby.' Father would, as Marguerite read, often take us on long walks and play with us outdoors.

And, Murray is also generous to acknowledge my mother, four years her husband's senior, Mary Penrose Arnold. As he mentions her, I have hope that she vaguely revives somewhere in the netherworld whenever people such as Marguerite read his book. I feel this to be true.

I was the eldest male sibling. My sister Jane, (renamed 'K' by my father), was the absolute oldest. As my brother Tom wrote, "when we are all at home, there is nothing but joking and fun from morning to night." Marguerite relished imagining having seven siblings and actually living with a dog named 'Spot.' The possibility of such a family life being real lifted her mood.

Murray's book contains a photo of our home at Fox How. The naturalness of the structure itself has to impress you. Stacked local stones make the gate. And a thick wood fence surrounds the property. The house is not only in the woods, it is *of* the woods. I love sports, especially tennis. My love of fishing and hunting, my relishing of long walks, all began in the woods around Fox How.

I think cramped urban spaces suffocate today's youth. As Marguerite drooled over my childhood home, I wondered how I might get her out into nature – to see some stars. "This would," I thought, "help her immensely."
Marguerite longed to be in Fox How with all us Arnolds. As she was struggling academically and already seventeen, she couldn't see herself as friends of Dr. Arnold or any of his children. So she imagined another mode of entry.

"Hello. I am here for the nanny position," she'd tell Mrs. Arnold. And, once inside, she would play with the children. She realized that, as an employee, she should be distant from the children; she was to chaperone. Somehow, though, she thought Dr. and Mrs. Arnold would indulge her playful managerial style. She was probably right.

As Murray's biography describes, we young Arnold sires enjoyed digging more than any other game. This factoid boggled Marguerite's mind. "Who today knows about such simple pleasures?" But, our precocious literary output impressed her more than anything else.

At fourteen, sister K wrote "The History of Jane's Life." As a team, we created a newspaper, the 'Fox How Magazine.' This little periodical ran twice a year from the time I was fifteen till I was nineteen.

Beyond the average person, Marguerite also felt amazement that William Wordsworth often visited Fox How. Poetry had been the one school subject that actually captured her fancy. As such, she had read a few poems by Wordsworth. And, of the many poems this budding artist wrote, several pathetically attempted to mimic his style.

Ultimately, I much preferred urbane city life to Fox How's rusticity. But, to Marguerite, this detail did not matter. 'Charming,' 'warm,' 'loving,' and 'ideal' were the words she used to describe the magic we experienced at Fox How; words, she noticed, that seemed alien to her.

As I did when reading her dossier, the enraptured young reader choked up as she read of the leg braces I wore from the age of two to four. My father dubbed me 'Crabby' because I walked much like a crab.

I, personally, cannot recall this endearing (apparently – at least to her) weakness. No one knows what caused me to walk strangely as a child. I never had physical problems beyond childhood. In fact, I even jumped over a fence the day before my death at age sixty-five. Still, I appreciated Marguerite's sentimentality over my leg irons.

My childhood delighted Marguerite. But, she could not help but get snared in contrasts between my childhood and hers. I wrote a letter to my mother every week of my life. In contrast, Marguerite's mother gave her up at birth and her adopted mother hadn't answered her phone calls in nearly two years.

Her nostalgia over my youth ultimately stemmed from her feeling abandoned.

"I have been ripped off. Not even my teachers know as much as the Arnold children did at the age of ten. My friends don't create newspapers and play with their fathers; they listen to suffocating loud screaming music and get stoned alone."

Though today, in her estimation, "sucked" by comparison, Murray's depiction of my quaint childhood provided some hope to my young ward – some evidence of the existence of beauty in the world.

CHAPTER
~ 5 ~

SUICIDE

The process by which we guides become apparent to our charges often frightens them. Marguerite felt my presence Monday in the library. She attributed the sensation to nerves. But she was positively startled as she saw my likeness reflected in a glazed window of a school door next to which I was standing.

Her heart leapt into her throat, she jerked backwards and gasped audibly. At that a student exclaimed, "Watch it Spaz." She hurriedly turned to see if anything behind her could have made the unlikely reflection of my tall sideburn-lined face appear in the window. There was nothing. She was spooked.

I don't know why we appear gradually to those we guide. It may simply reflect the material realities of the connection between the material and spiritual worlds. But, I believe that the slight startles allow those we help to acclimate to our presence. This way, when we finally get unveiled, the person doesn't go insane from fright.

By the way, we do not have any choice concerning when or how strongly we show to the living. I am thrust into the world without warning. And, once in it, I must lurk and wait until fully visible to my charge. But, I can also fade away, unseen, without notice. My appearance is that tenuous.

On Tuesday, Marguerite saw my shadow on a wall. It appeared near the floor for two solid minutes of her biology class. She recognized me via the part in my hair and sideburns in the silhouette.

She wanted to scream. But screaming inside the classroom would not make her popular. She worried that she was losing her mind. And, I don't think my emphatically waving 'hello' helped her feel less insane in any way.

At this point, though, poor Marguerite was so close to suicide that my ghostly appearance just came as one more of many disturbances. Over stimulated and lost in a daze, in a very real sense she hardly registered my appearance consciously.

I was conscious of being near Marguerite and monitoring her feelings both when I appeared in the door window and when I appeared on the wall. But, I drifted into these situations only minutes before she crossed my path and went back into the fog – so to speak – very shortly after the episodes ended.

It is frustrating, but we guides often see the world in these sorts of snippets. As such, we often only have the dossiers, and not much more, to go on as we do our guiding work.

If you're listening, powers-that-be, this is a severe disadvantage.

The amount of lingering I had been allowed on this assignment was unprecedented. Being able to watch her for so long in the library, and being able to listen to some of her ruminations, I thought I had come to understand her. Having such extended periods of consciousness was a pure joy. But worry muddled this purity. Had I been allowed to maintain my presence because my odds of saving her were not so great?

The evening of the same day that I appeared on her school wall, I faded into consciousness standing in front of Marguerite's home. I knew it was her home because after only waiting two minutes, she came out of it. Her leaving the main door ajar, not looking back at the slamming screen door, and the pace at which she shot out of the house, conveyed a mood of extreme upset. I was panicked.

I quickly intuited that she had written a suicide note. In it, she spoke of noise, people and fatigue. My impressions of the sources of her malady were accurate.

I knew this was the day; this was the moment. I had to act. But she still couldn't see me and I had no idea where she was headed.

Sobbing, Marguerite stopped at a freeway overpass and looked down. Her intentions became clear. As she lifted a leg on the railing, I tried to stop her but my hand slipped through her body. A split moment later, she stood, fully erect and swayed on the overpass barrier.

At last, in blind anxiety I screamed, "Marguerite, don't do it!"

At the surprising sound of my call, Marguerite screamed. As she did so, her elbows bent and her hands went over her shoulders, her back stiffened. The scream propelled her head back. And, thankfully, this caused her to fall, backwards. She hit the sidewalk with a hard sharp thud and hardly registered the pain before frantically crawling backwards.

"Where the fuck did you come from?" She stared at me in horror.

"Don't kill yourself!" I pleaded, approaching with my hands forward.

She screamed again and crawled further backwards. "Don't touch me! Have you been following me? Are you some sort of . . ." And then silence. "Matthew Arnold?" She incredulously uttered.

"At your service, Marguerite." I bowed with a touch of curtsy, showing completely inappropriate affect.

"How? Who?"

"Well Dear, it's complicated, but I, Matthew Arnold, have been sent as your guide from the spirit realm."

"Sent from . . ?"

"Yes, from life after death."

"If there is life after death, I want to go there now, I want to get out of this fucking world." She scurried to her feet and pointed over the railing.
"Wait, it is not as simple as that My Heart. Yes, life continues after death. But, you only get to remember what you did and what has been said of you. If you kill yourself

now you'll only have your sad seventeen years to remember."

"So fucking what!"

"Until you fade, you'll feel the pain of your father every day until he dies."

She stared at me blankly.

"Frozen lamentation is all there is for you on the other side. You have much beauty to cultivate. You mustn't take the journey to the other side yet."

At that Marguerite turned and ran. She actually ran through the left side of my body. She cried the whole way home.

Emotions pulsated through me. My body shook and I was disturbed by my inability to breathe. I couldn't stop thinking about poor Marguerite, what I did right and what I might have said differently. It took about ten minutes for me to calm my body and stop obsessing over what had just transpired. It took me another five to realize I was on the earth and had time.

My mission had been accomplished. In every other occasion in which I had been sent to prevent suicide, I would have immediately faded afterwards. Yet curiously, I had not disappeared. I took this to mean that, she was not out of danger – that she still had suicidal tendencies.

But, with time, and Marguerite nowhere in sight, I found I had nothing to do. I manifested paper and wrote the previous chapters.

CHAPTER
~ 6 ~

DARKNESS AND LIGHT

Deviously, Marguerite smiled and waved to her father as she left her home the day after her aborted suicide attempt. She was pretending that she was going to school; She had no such intention. I understood. The day after a suicide attempt one must have a lot on their mind.

To get to school, she turned left at the main street and kept walking straight for about twenty minutes. But, today, after the left, she took the first right. She went down about four blocks and turned right again, on another street crowded with cars.

Her father did not drive this way to work. She felt safe. And, as this direction took her away from the freeway overpass, I felt safe too.

As I approached her, I sensed that the young urchin felt much less pain than she had the night before. The mystery of my appearance, with a new knowledge that the universe might care, added some curiosity to her mind. As Newton taught us, no two objects can occupy the same space at the same time. Confusion and a hint of excitement, replaced some of her pain.

I had no idea how she would react to me, but I wanted to make my presence known.

"Hello, Dear," I waved from about five feet behind her.

She turned and looked at me with a fearful expression of vexed curiosity. "Dearest, I don't wish to intrude, but I am your guide and my job is to spend time by your side. I do hope you'll find my company tolerable. I mean you no harm and I am occasionally fun and funny!" I capped off my speech with a bow and large smile meant to ingratiate.

"First of all," She began, "I want to thank you for what you did for me last night on the overpass."

"You, Dear, are entirely welcome. It was my not only my duty, but my honor as well. And, might I add that I too owe you a modicum of gratitude." I approached her tentatively, stopping before she might consider my proximity menacing.

"How come?" She asked, nonplussed by my jerky, unsure movements.

"I do not get called to guide very often anymore." I said with a touch of melancholy.

"Is that 'cause no one remembers you any more?"

"No, they do, Love, they do." I straightening myself defensively, showing pride in my reputation, "In fact, this year saw a book published on me, several titles that featured me, as well as appearances in many articles, in prestigious journals, nonetheless."

"But, . . . ?"

"But the people who write these are not desperate. They write safely and successfully within the academy. They have no need of guidance."

"And, I do!?" Marguerite shot back, sensitive to slights.

"Well, yes, Love, you do! And, there is another factor as well." I murmured with a sympathetic grin. "People searching, people liable to get lost, no longer read me. In the early 1950s, I used to be a cultural touchstone and guide troubled souls twice a year. I haven't been back to earth since the early 1960s."

"Well I've only read your stuff for a few weeks," she somberly admitted with her eyes on her feet.

"Then My Young Darling, you must be an exceptional study. You have an open soul. One that can be touched by beauty." I took care not mention her desperation again. At that, Marguerite's shyness produced a blush.

"At any rate, Love," I continued, "I appreciate whatever efforts you made to conjure me." She moved her arm to invite me to walk with her. I nodded and scampered up to her side.

Our voices are, it occurred to me, stark contrasts. Marguerite's voice has very little in the way of lilt. It is

cool and subdued – the sound of shy depression, her voice rang monotone. I consciously work towards singing my words; I find it enjoyable.
Marguerite, had never heard such a voice. Her father had a certain lightness to his words that came from his constant desire to conciliate. My tonal quality comes from clarity of purpose. I am not only excited; I wish to be heard, as such I over annunciate.

"Do you always call people, 'Dear', and, 'Love.'?" She asked.

"Oh, yes, Sweetness." I smiled, "Kindness and politeness are integral parts of civilization, the very essence of sweetness and light."

Marguerite's furrowing and slight smirk let me know that she had no idea what I was talking about, but found it amusing.

"Charm is so very important, isn't it?" I finished, standing erect as though I were posing for a painting.

Then turning very serious, she asked, "Should I tell you, you being my guide and all, what pushed me over the edge?"

"Well, Love, you needn't. But if it will make you feel better."

At this, anticipatory emotion swelled my chest and eyes. In life, I was quite stoic. My family history, I had always known, predisposed me to an early death; My father and his father before him died young. And, when my father died suddenly at the age of forty-six, I spoke to no one about my feelings. Even, the death of three of my children found me publicly unshaken. But, since dying myself, I have become uncontrollably emotional.

"Shall we sit?" I asked gesturing towards a bench in a glass box.

"At a bus bench?" She asked, with an incredulous expression.

"No?" I asked sincerely, not knowing if this was inappropriate.

"Well okay," she conceded, "it's just a little strange."

"Stranger than speaking to Matthew Arnold?" I mused.

"Yeah. I guess you got me there." After sitting, she began, "There was a party last night. And, as usual, everyone got pretty wasted. Actually," she made sure to tell me, "I didn't because I don't smoke or drink. But there were about fifteen people in Harlan's house. He's my boyfriend's friend. They were all pretty wasted.

"The party got pretty wild. We all started making out." And reading the clue on my face, she detailed, "That means kissing with our tongues." Giving words to my reaction of slight nausea, she excitedly editorialized, "The whole scene seemed like a bucket of snakes to me."

"Anyhow, Ricky, my boyfriend, and I were kissing pretty heavily. And he started to take my shirt off. I said, 'No!' I mean we were in a room of people. And, he said, 'look, everyone is doing it.' And, he was right. As I looked around the room, three girls were topless – including my best friend Philina. But, I thought the entire event was creepy. I didn't know where it was going, I mean . . . Can I tell you a secret?"

"Yes, Love," I calmly replied with a tilt of the head, though not really wishing to hear more.
"I'm a virgin. I haven't, you know, done it."

"Okay," I replied, both stunned that a young female would share that sort of information with me and by the fact Marguerite perceived virginity as some sort of scandalous secret.

"Well, I held my ground. I told Ricky, 'No.' And, all of a sudden he stands up and he said, in front of everybody, 'You know what? Forget you. You're a fucking bummer and a cock tease and you give me attitude whenever I'm playing my video games. You're a fuckin' loser bitch.'

"And, I told him, 'You know what, you're a fucking dog and a follower. You pretend to be so tough. But, I know you, Enrique. I know you have feelings.' And at that he did something I thought he'd never do, he hit me."

At that I couldn't take it any more and I began to weep copiously. "No. No. Mr. Arnold, don't. It's okay. Mr. Arnold."

"I'm sorry Dear, it's just so horrible," I said, fighting to stop myself from being emotional. "You're a beautiful young intellectual being and the horrors you've been subjected to, . . . I can't listen to anymore, I'm sorry."

"No, no. That's it. That's the whole story."

"I'm sorry. It's too much for me, Love. I come from another era where not even the most rank and low people, would consider behaving in such a vile and animalistic way. It is as if people have descended into the pits of venality and merit nothing so much as, as to be, to be . . . killed."

"No. It's not like that, Ricky is a sweetheart deep down. He just is . . ."

"Stop. You've got to stop. Ricky is hopeless. You need to spend time with people that are worthy of you, people that appreciate beauty and seek to cultivate it in themselves. And, if that means being alone forever . . . Look," I said looking as seriously into her eyes as I have ever looked into anyone's, "never degrade yourself. I am glad you stood up for yourself when necessary. But you mustn't put yourself near people like that again."

"But, Ricky . . ."

"It isn't safe!" I angrily exclaimed.

That hit home. I could tell because she sat up straight and then slumped forward as if admitting a truth and giving up fighting it.

"Yeah, you're right. It isn't. And, after dealing with Ricky, I get so tired of this world and all the fuckin' shit in it. He drove me to trying to kill myself. And, if you hadn't a shown up . . ."

"Beauty exists, Love. Good people exist. Respect exists. You don't need to curry favor with unevolved beings."

Marguerite looked down at her hands. She was quiet. Just then a bus pulled up and set a few destitute-looking souls free. At the sight of them, she saw me instinctively shudder and grimace. She smiled at this judgmental wickedness.

"Dearest, My Love, can we walk?"

"Yeah?" She replied looking at me with a tilted head, that seemed to ask, 'How can a person be so affected?' To which I smiled a reassuring smile, and took a deep faux breath, brushed my hair back, stood up and strode forward.

When she had caught up to me and my long strides, I told her the sad urgent truth, "Darling, I hate to say it, but as soon as you're out of trouble, I'll likely disappear."

"Really!" She gasped with concern I found flattering.

"Yes, My Darling Heart, but it is nothing personal. I mean, I have no control over it. In fact, I am amazed that I am still here. The longest I've ever spent with anyone was half an hour and we've already met twice."

"I see," she somberly uttered with downcast eyes.

"No, Dear, you don't. My point is that life is very short. We must be fully appreciative of the moments of consciousness we have. And, I have found that this appreciation is best expressed in proper conduct. Conduct is four-fifths of life, you know?" I smiled very pleased to be quoting myself.

"And the other fifth?" She asked.

"Dairy, actually milk," I announced with dry humor that confused her, "But that is not important now." I smiled a beaming smile. "We must always be composed and show an appreciation for each other and civilization."

"Isn't that fake?" She earnestly asked.

'Or the poet who sings you so well?
Is it you, O beauty, O grace,
O charm, O romance, that we feel,
Or the voice which reveals what you are?'

I offered, quoting my poem, 'The Youth of Nature,' with broad gestures. This, I am proud to say, momentarily took young Marguerite's breath away. While the meaning eluded my young charge, she perfectly synched with its spirit.

"Darling, all is fake. Look, civilization is artifice. And, don't worry; The sadness will come. And, you'll not be boring due to an abundance of bliss. But, awareness of death and real appreciation for life, is shown in elegant conduct, being careful for, and appropriate to, the fragility of all we have."

"So, I should act like you?"

"Well, not smiling is rude. So, at very least, My Love, you could try smiling. It would make me feel so much better."

At that Marguerite managed a hint of a smile. "Ah, my guidance has been worthwhile," I beamed, dramatically clasping my hands next to my chest. At that she gave even more of a hint of a smile. In fact, if scientists studied it, I believe they would be able to prove that she actually did smile.

"Let's have some fun, shall we? Would you permit me to discuss a poem with you?"

"Yes, I'd love to, it would be an honor." She said with an expectant yet unsure demeanor.
"You make an old man's heart soar, My Love. Thank you."

"I'm going to the mall." She said pointing to an enormous structure that reminded me of the whale that swallowed Jonah.

"I'll meet you inside of that mall then."

"In the food court." She beamed, "Third floor."

At that I smiled, nodded, and started running down the street towards the structure. I hadn't had the opportunity to run, skip and jump in so long. I had been wishing to do so ever since I had first appeared in Marguerite's life. Now that I had some assurance that my young charge was safe, and I could stay for a bit, I indulged my playful spirit. I ran through the shrubberies, and down the grass strips, all the way to the 'mall.'

CHAPTER

~ 7 ~

POETRY

'White,' is a good word to describe Marguerite's mall. 'Antiseptic,' is another. And if these words describe the mall as a whole, they seem particularly apt for the 'food court.' I found it not without relevance that 'white' and 'antiseptic' also describe a toilet. The mall's white motif serves as a canvas to show off the products the mall sells. I'll leave it to you to complete the toilet analogy.

All considered, I took great delight in the privilege of striding through the corridors and looking at the shops. None of the displayed clothes came close to the elegance of mine: a three-piece suit with trousers of a seal-brown check, a double breasted jacket and vest, woven in many colors, with gold buttons, topped off by a cerulean pocket scarf, flecked with cherry.

In over one hundred years of guiding, I had never had such an expanse of time. As such, I felt relaxed, and especially dandy, as I strode past the shops. I didn't need to cram words of wisdom in, as I had done just earlier. I could guide slowly. At least I hoped I could.

"Mr. Arnold, Mr. Arnold," These joyous words directed my attention to Marguerite waving from a table across the crowd. I appreciated both her enthusiasm for me and her willingness to read my poetry, (at least until she got bored). What a delightful youth this Marguerite was. It seemed to me incongruous that she could be depressed. But, I understand too well that gaiety and misery can exist side by side.

"Mr. Arnold," she queried as I sat, "Do you go by the name Matt or Matthew sometimes?"

"With my peers, Darling. But, you're a youth and my charge. It would be inappropriate for us to parade as equals, at least not this week," I grinned. "But, occasional terms of affection preceding my name would not hurt."

"All right my dearest Mr. Arnold!" She smirked and rolled her eyes up at me, up through her dreadfully collapsed posture – her stringy hair hanging straight down and nearly touching her jeans.

"Speaking of authority, I am a poet of some repute. But, do you know what I did for a day job?"

"School inspector?"

"Oh, yes - the worst drudgery. But, I wanted to let you know that it hadn't escaped my notice that this is a school day."

At that Marguerite's posture got even worse.

"But Dear, I only mention it as a matter of fact – as a matter of honesty. I can take joy in your taking a day or two off. Remember I am 'playing hooky,' as you Americans might still say, from death." And at that I smiled regally and checked, only to see that her reaction had risen to flatness.

"You're crazy. I don't get you. You are so formal, and yet you were nearly flipping across the grass and through the parking lot. I love it. But, I can't quite figure out if you're nuts or what's up."

"Dearest, conduct, . . ."

"Four-fifths?"

"Give or take a fraction," I affirmed, "is civilized play; playing at royalty. Certainly, you did such things as a child – play, run across parking lots, pretend you lived in castles and bow a lot. After some time, if you continuously cultivate such a sense of play, you'll find expansive thoughts and feelings come to you as naturally as your current slouching demeanor and posture."

Taking my point, she sat up. And I placed my fingers at the side of my mouth to indicate a smile. She involuntarily smirked and released a single muffled chortle, which she tried to pass off as a cough.

"Good enough." I grinned with my teeth displayed in all their ruddiness. I do so love affect. With a smile one can deliver comments that are brutally honest or even cutting, without hurt feelings. This tact had made my correction of

Marguerite's posture go down well. When cruel, nothing beats a smile.

"So let's play, 'read the poem.'" Marguerite offered, entering into the swing of things.

"Are we going to read, 'To Marguerite'?"

"Yes!"

"I assume that you know the background story."

"I know that you fell in love while traveling in Switzerland and that it didn't work out."

"'It didn't work out.' You Americans enjoy such practical relationships. When I was last guiding, in the 1950s, your nation assumed the republican virtue of fidelity to spouses and family rearing. The people I helped mostly had families. But, now relationships run as long as flames, they last as long as, as, umm . . . help me Dear, I'm stuck."

"As long as video games?"

"Sure. Thank you, Love. As long as video games."

Marguerite smirked from between her hair.

"And, please excuse my lecturing. It is an occupational hazard for a social critic."

"No. Not at all. I enjoy it. It's new; it's something I haven't heard before. You're a freak. I mean, um, in a good way," she defensively backtracked. "I mean, yes, please continue."

"Yes, quite the freak." I smiled broadly, fanning my fingers out and displaying my hands' backsides. "When I was young, I met an enchanting phantom, so the story goes, named Marguerite. And, she became, for me, a symbol of loss, of passion and youth. And, an entire series of my poems used her as a symbol."

"But, she wasn't just a symbol. She was real, wasn't she?"

"Oh wouldn't you like to know," I smiled, relishing the intrigue.

"Well, what happened? Why didn't you . . . work out?"

"Some have read class into our ultimate disenchantment, she was poor. And that is in the poems."

"Class! How disgusting." Marguerite exclaimed.

"Yes." I replied looking down. "I agree. But, herein class only stands for levels of fluidity with certain circles. A woman such as Marguerite would not work in London's high society. Different circles, different tastes, different worlds. We'd be as odd in hers as she'd be in ours."

"I see."

"But, she also just became a pure ideal. Her being unattainable, as with all chivalrous love, only fed my love for her. And, it fed on itself. The poem expresses the distance between the real and the ideal, between what we want and what we really can get."

"So the poem, 'To Marguerite,' really isn't just about Marguerite."

"Yes, that's true, My Blooming Heart. The poem really concerns the limits of this." At that, I dramatically swung my arms out to gesture at all of the many people scattered around the food court.

"But enough blather, let's look at the poem." And then with a devious raising of my eyebrows, I asked, "Did you know that I can materialize paper, pen and poems?"

"No really?"

"Yes, it is one of the few parlor tricks my being a ghost affords. It isn't much, but it amuses me. Watch!" And at that, a copy of my poem simply appeared in my hand.

"Wow!" My young companion uttered, "If someone ever tried to rob you, you could make the complete three volume collection of all your writing appear and wollop 'em with it!"

I threw my head back in near silent laughter as she gurgled, "Quite, Dear, quite! At any rate, here she is:"

To Marguerite

YES! in the sea of life enisl'd,
With echoing straits between us thrown,
Dotting the shoreless watery wild,
We mortal millions live *alone*.
The islands feel the enclasping flow,
And then their endless bounds they know.

But when the moon their hollows lights,
And they are swept by balms of spring,
And in their glens, on starry nights,
The nightingales divinely sing;
And lovely notes, from shore to shore,
Across the sounds and channels pour —

Oh! then a longing like despair
Is to their farthest caverns sent;
For surely once, they feel, we were
Parts of a single continent!
Now round us spreads the watery plain —
Oh might our marges meet again!

Who order'd, that their longing's fire
Should be, as soon as kindled, cool'd?
Who renders vain their deep desire?
— A God, a God their severance rul'd!
And bade betwixt their shores to be
The unplumb'd, salt, estranging sea.

"You know," Marguerite confessed," I read this poem before and I liked the part about 'us mortals living alone.' But I didn't get details at all, like what does enisl'd' mean?"

"It means, on an island, 'enisl'd'"

"Oh, yeah, duh, I see it. We all live, like on islands. I see small islands, all far apart separated by too much water. I see it. As I walk through my classes and my school hallways, even when I'm with my friends, I sometimes feel totally alone, like I'm on an island. Sometimes, I think that has to do with my being adopted. Did you know that I'm adopted?"

"Yes. I do, Dearest."
"How do you know?"

"I received a dossier on you – a small report. I have your basic information. But, I only know what you know about you, nothing more."

"Interesting."

"And perhaps your orphaned state does account for your resonance with me. Many of my poems concerned loneliness. I even wrote a poem about an adopted son meeting his father, 'Sohrab and Rustum.'" Perhaps not wishing to discuss her adoption, Marguerite turned back to the poem. I sat in silence as she scrutinized the magic paper.

"Ah, then I see it, I think I see it. In the second paragraph we feel a possibility of connection. Like we can hear birds signing, from island to island."

'The nightingales divinely sing;
And lovely notes, from shore to shore,
Across the sounds and channels pour —'

"Yes, and the nightingales often serve as a symbol for love. So, yes, under the dark starred sky, at a distance, we can sometimes feel love from each other. We feel connection with each other, from our separate islands."

"So beautiful," She murmured still searching the page. "Okay let me read the third one so I can see if I can get it." She pensively looked it over with a couple of involuntary thought-processing sounds.

"What do you observe, Love?"
"Well, we feel despair because, as sure as we love, as sure as we all, at some level, feel connected, we also feel our separation."

"Yes, precisely. And, I have read a lot about Hinduism and reincarnation. And that has helped me see our souls as one. But, paradoxically, that has just made me more aware of how separate we all are."

"Oh my God, I love it. So amazing."

She mouthed the words:

For surely once, they feel, we were

Parts of a single continent!

Now round us spreads the watery plain —

Oh might our marges meet again!

And, after a pause, she asked with a furrow, "I guess the line, 'Parts of a single continent' refers to when all the continents were all one. Right? And 'marges' refers to Marguerite."

"Well, yes, 'single continent' refers to Pangea."

"Yeah, that's the name, I couldn't remember it."

"Pangea. And, yes, 'marges' does refer to Margue . . . your name." I smiled. "But it also refers to 'marges,' meaning where the land meets the seashore. This makes it a place where different elements mix, like land, water, and air (not to mention social classes). Aaaand," I stressed, proud of my many layers of meaning, "the divided continents also refer to the actual channel between England and Switzerland, the English Channel, which separates my nation from Marguerite's continent. Aaaand it also refers to something totally different. You see in my time, religion was dying."

"Yeah, cool!" She cheered.

"Dear, why on earth would you celebrate the death of religion?"

"I don't know. It's repressive and hypocritical?" She queried.

"Okay, Love, perhaps we'll discuss that later. But, in my time, I found the disappearance sad. Religion bound our nation together and joined our nation to other nations. It gave us a common worldview, respect for each other as souls. But, science smashed that. Reincarnation is not real. So, the distance between our souls doesn't just allude to me and Marguerite; it is a symbol of the West's ongoing cultural situation. With the rise of science we became machines, with no common beliefs to unite us."

"How beautiful, again. I didn't know a poem could do so much."

"Thank you Love, for your appreciation. It is appreciated. Okay, on to the final stanza with you."

Again, she mouthed the words:

**Who order'd, that their longing's fire
Should be, as soon as kindled, cool'd?
Who renders vain their deep desire?
— A God, a God their severance rul'd!
And bade betwixt their shores to be
The unplumb'd, salt, estranging sea.**

"And, so it is God that separated us? No, 'A God,' not God. God wouldn't – from what you said – want us separate. What could separate us? Oh, maybe . . . could the God that separates us be science? You're calling science a new God?"

"Could be! Could very likely be." I as good as affirmed, "It is what separated all of us, now that God has been displaced, by way of a salty sea. And that's why it's unplumbed. Science doesn't investigate loneliness. And, the salty refers to something that will only make us thirstier by drinking it. And, I fear, the more we identify with science and its products, the less connected we'll feel. Science robs us of spiritual connections to others and ourselves. The resulting deep loss feels much like the yearning separation I felt from Marguerite. Like we're in a soulless, loveless world."

"I like it very much, Mr. Arnold, very much. I can feel the cultural, personal and romantic loneliness all mixed together."

"Thank you, Dearest."

"Wow. So was Marguerite real? A lot of people write about that."

"Did you know that I forbade that any biography of me be written?"

"That isn't answering the question, is it? You won't tell me, will you?"

"My work isn't about me. Even if there is some autobiographical reference, a poem shouldn't just refer to one's particular inconsequential life. 'To Marguerite' is about the rise of science and the death of God in the modern age – and the longing that causes. Cultivating a critical distance from the sordid details of our own lives is a part of wisdom, a sign of intelligence. We see things better from a distance. I look at history and nations. I, personally, myself, am not that interesting."

"You are to me!"

"Well, bless you Sweetness. Okay, I'll tell you who Marguerite was. Ready?"

"Yes."

"Marguerite was my neighbor's dog. I loved that old sow to pieces!"

"Mr. Arnold!"

"What? Animal love is the highest form of love there is."

"Eww."

"Darling, pleaaase your mind is so filthy. I meant that I love animals as much as people. And, if it will make the poem more meaningful, please always imagine my Marguerite as a playful loyal pup, who loved to have her belly scratched. That's who I wanted connection with. 'Ah Marguerite, I miss her smell!'" I swooned, hands clutch by my cheek.

At that we both laughed. It was great to see Marguerite laugh. She had spent far too much of her life rolled up, knees to chest, paralyzed by tangled ideas weighing her down.

"Marguerite, I have something to tell you."

"Yes." She clasped her hands dutifully in her lap and sat up straight.

"I want you to know that I have an instinctual feeling that I might get to spend a bit of time with you."

"I'd like that."

"I say that cautiously because I might disappear, as I said, at any moment and never come back. But, I have been allowed to linger with you much longer than I have ever been allowed to stay with anyone. And, I feel you're out of danger and I'm still here."

"I do feel much better. Thanks to you. I have some new insights on life. I feel like the world I took so seriously, my world, means a little less to me. *In a good way!*" She hastened to clarify.

"That is exactly what I was talking about moments ago. Yes, look at the world and spend less time considering our personal situation. This allows us to see the world as it really is." Marguerite was bobbing her head in rapt attention. For fun, I stopped and bobbed my head in rhythm with her. Then we did a little head-bobbing dance. She needed a little levity and I was able to provide it.

"I can't believe that I got to run across the park. It is amazing. I am happy to say, I think we'll meet again, Sweetness. But please do remember our happy times, always, when I finally go."

I reached out and attempted to put my hand on hers. But, I slid right through her hand and the table. It always seemed inappropriate and brutal, that when I returned I couldn't touch humans – other than in their hearts.

"Islands all, separated by salty seas," She sighed, looking right into my eyes.

And at that, I began to fade. And, as I did I tried to send her a broad reassuring smile. But, I don't think she saw it. While no longer visible to her, I saw her furrow her brows, make a pouty face, cross her legs and arms, and slouch. I had some work to do with this one.

Then she noticed that the poem had remained. She picked it up, began to read it and smiled ever so slightly at the corners of her mouth.

CHAPTER
~ 8 ~

ARNOLD GOES TO SCHOOL

The next day I appeared in Marguerite's school hallway as she strolled towards her English class. I waved at her and psychically said, 'Hello.' She was startled.

"Yes Darling, I can speak to you psychically. And, on a good day, I can go into your mind and read your thoughts a bit. But, don't worry, you can fight and kick me out, if you don't trust me. Also, at some point you may have the wonderful fortune of entering my thoughts! Oh you are such a lucky young lady."

"Actually," Marguerite replied walking towards class, (seeing me constantly at about ten feet in front of her floating backwards – students' bodies going effortlessly through mine), "if I were given the ability to enter anyone else's head and see what was going on, it might be yours.

Though I also often wonder what the hell my father is thinking too."

Marguerite's calm was quite amazing. Having gotten used to the unlikely actuality of my existence, my floating in front of her and speaking with her psychically didn't perturb her.

Though I could, and would, read their minds, I had never spoken to a charge entirely psychically before. It would, I assumed, scare them. This was getting interesting. Being allowed to linger and establish a relationship with my charge, gave me leeway for exploration.

Now, Dear Reader, I don't know if you have noticed, but I have a wicked sense of humor. I used to tell dignified Oxford scholars that my friends were mental defectives under my charge. At first my friends resented the implication of their mental feebleness. But, before very long, I got the whole group drooling and grunting with delight. I started looking around for a prank I might play with Marguerite.

We entered her classroom and sat down. It was a rich environment. So many books and posters lined the wall! The impoverished East London children whose schools I monitored would hardly believe a classroom could be so decorative.

"Isn't it simply marvelous that your literature books still contain my poems?" I asked, sitting just next to Marguerite. As I weigh nothing, bending as if I were sitting or even reclining, without a chair, takes no effort at all.

"Sure it is." Marguerite silently replied in her nonplussed school mode.

"Dead now over one hundred and twenty five years, and I still pervade the culture. Tell me that isn't simply marvelous."

With a slight irritation she repeated, "Yes! It's marvelous." And, yes! I did it! I had caught her. I said, 'marvelous,' at the very same time she did. In doing so, I was able to synch up with her thoughts, to gain some control.

"I mean it's a . . . What the hell!" Just then I made Marguerite's hand jut up in the air.

"Play with me Marguerite! Let's have fun!"

"Mr. . . . uh, uh, . . . " I spoke through her, using her voice.

"Early!" Marguerite supplied somewhat angrily.

"Mr. Early, have you thought about Matthew Arnold's relation to modernism? Could you lecture to us about that topic?"

"I have no idea what you're talking about."

"Could you at least take a stab at it? What did Victorian-era poets generally think about the modern world?"

"Um, I mostly read modern poetry. It speaks to me."

"Well, that is all too sad. You constantly call poetry a mode of self-expression, but you don't recognize how modern and limited a vision that is. Perhaps if you spent more time exploring history, (and less on poetry that you think celebrates you), you'd understand the changing functions of poetry over time a bit more; you could relate poetry to society; you could teach with a historical orientation."

At that moment, Marguerite looked around the room and felt something she had never felt before, *snobbery*. It felt good. Philina's head was propped up on her chin with an expression that combined 'Who cares?' with disdain. She was still upset about Marguerite's fighting with Ricky at the party a few nights earlier.

For the first time Marguerite noticed how much Philina looked like a cow chewing cud. She let out a haughty single-syllable laugh, "Ha!" At which time Philina rolled her eyes, gave us a dirty look and turned to look at Mr. Early.

"Well Ms. Smarty Pants," Mr. Early scowled, "if you think that topic is so important, perhaps you could write a ten-page paper on it."

Mr. Early's threat was meant to shut her up. And, Marguerite, in turn, told me to shut up. But, I had heard this sort of tactic from teachers before and deplored it more than I deplored anything. "The fact that you use intellectual exploration as a threat is disgusting!" I exclaimed, through Marguerite.

"Ms. Buckby," Mr. Early shot angrily. Did you just say what I thought I heard you say? You're this close to getting sent to the Principal." He projected a very serious expression while holding his finger and thumb an inch apart at eye level.

Under her breath, Marguerite told me to stop. But, she put up noticeably little resistance when I continued. She was both terrified and thrilled at her new understanding and rebellion. My confidence carried both of us.

"Mr. Early, why have you never brought what you're reading or writing into the classroom? Surely, to write is to know one's own mind for the first time. With more exertion Sir, you could be a significant intellectual role model and introduce us to the life of the mind. Having us write our autobiographies and cut 'n' paste mini-biographies over and over again is . . ."

"I've had enough of you!" Mr. Early screamed, outraged. "You're going to the Principal's office right now." At that he started nervously looking through his desk drawer for the referral slip.

"A fine reply to a cry for intellectual engagement. Send me off. Who knows? It might improve your school's test scores." In my day they tried to institute a 'pay for performance' program. I had long resented using test scores to judge schools and teachers.

"Oh, it would!" He replied, with his attention still on finding the referral paper, "If I only could send half of you damned morons . . ." He stopped abruptly, but it had already been said. The class moaned and hooted. And, at this moment Marguerite felt badly for Mr. Early. He had just sunk the rest of the semester.

This sad man did not want to be there. My poetic gift seized, around the age of thirty-one, when I got married. But I then switched from poetry to writing essays – to social and literary criticism and such. Though no longer passionate enough for poetry, I kept my mind fully engaged. I had a reason to live.

Mr. Early had sensed finer things. He had worshipped at the poetic muse's alter. And when his poetry led to nothing, when he took his day job, something inside of

him also died. Finding no other outlet, the talent inside him rotted and festered until it turned to venom. With his venomous comment, he poisoned his class.
"Mr. Early." Marguerite yelled from her desk, totally on her own, "I am sorry Sir. This was my fault." Her sense of empathy made me emotional.

Mr. Early didn't look up as filled in his form, "Well it's too late for that." Then listlessly again, as if speaking to himself, he echoed the phrase "It's too late now."

"What was that?!" Marguerite yelped at me. "Now I am going to get in so much trouble! So much! I thought you were here as a my guide and now you're getting me in so much trouble, so much more trouble than I am already in – and that's a lot."

"Relax, you know you loved it." Then, with an enigmatic flip of the wrist and a glance to my upper left, I exclaimed, "*Snobbery*!"

"But Mr. Arnold," she pouted in a little girl way that was very unbecoming.

"I know I was naughty. But sometimes you just have to laugh and that was fun." And speaking to her empathy, I continued, "And whatever disappointments led Mr. Early to this sad state, he should not be teaching. He needs his students to challenge him, to hear a little truth. Who knows? If he takes today's meltdown to heart, he could be rejuvenated, perhaps even reengage with his muse. But until then, has not earned the sacrosanct title of 'teacher.'"

"Still," She wondered, packing her backpack, "what am I going to tell my father? I could get kicked out of school! I am failing two classes already and don't have the best attendance record. How could you, a guide, get me in so much trouble?"

"Well, I have no idea why they sent me to guide you in particular or why I am still here shadowing you." I had to watch my conduct as the excitement of the confrontation was still pulsating through my veins.

As she picked up her filled-out referral form from Mr. Early, Marguerite wore a glum, downcast face and looked at the floor. She said nothing as we left the classroom, and continued looking down as we started down the empty hallway towards the principal's office.

"Look," I changed tracks, "my father died at the age of forty-six of a heart attack, as his father did at fifty-six. I always lived with an awareness of death." This had Marguerite's attention. "That is why I can't convince myself that this little episode in your life is," I stated with a mock dramatic gesture to my forehead, and one eye on her, "*so very important.*"

This was the first time that Marguerite really felt my pathos. My father's death hurt and so sometimes I laugh too much. I love laughing. But, melancholy often shadows my glib remarks. She smiled sadly at me, as if to comfort me. But her thoughts remained very serious and largely focused on herself.

Then I could feel thoughts of suicide rising up in her mind. I moved in front of her. She stopped and looked at me with great worry. Having nothing to say, I blurted out, "Life is too short. You think you're in trouble? I'm dead! Damn it. Dead! This is not important. Damn it Dear, have a sense of humour!" And, with this, pulling back my anger, I nervously forced the biggest smile I could render. "Please?"

"Why Mr. Arnold," My cheering charge said with a southern accent, while bending her wrist, "Such language!" Though she still didn't know if explaining the perspective of a dead man would calm her father down, we both nearly formed dimples with our knowing smiles as we almost skipped down the empty halls towards the principal's office.

Then Marguerite suddenly stopped, "If anyone saw me talking to you, they would think I was . . ." And before she could finish the sentence she realized how much of her communication to me transpired silently.

And miming a deranged figure, with spastic arms, I uttered, "Mad as a hatter. I am seeing poets. Help me. Heeeeeelp me." This was fun and it emphasized that no one could see any of my madness. I was invisible. We were fairly safe. She only appeared to be giggling at an inside joke she was telling herself.

Marguerite stopped at her locker and took out *A Gift Imprisoned*, by Ian Hamilton. This book claims I became unpoetic and useless past the age of thirty-one. Unpoetic, okay; But useless? I wrote more on education and religion than any other Victorian writer – all past the age of thirty-one. And, I wrote up until the day I died. Please!

I had time to critique Hamilton's book because Marguerite was stalling, not wanting to turn the corner that led to the corridor with the principal's office and the guilty verdict.

"Have you seen the 1940 movie 'Tom Brown's School Days'?" I queried.

"Well, I never thought I'd hear you ask about movies, Mr. A."

"There is a very good 1940 version on youtube."

"Mr. A, surfs the web!!!"

"Well I wasn't born yesterday," I winked, "And, 'Mr. A?' Really? We'll have a discussion about that young lady."

"Okay Mr. A!" She replied. I liked this cheeky little girl.

"Well yes, youtube. I in fact have the best internet connection in the universe, it's psychic like. I automatically see all that still goes on in the world that pertains to me and that film gets some views yet! "And," I added, putting my head back with enjoyment, "This movie about my father's school was a biiiiiiiig hit."

Because Marguerite did not smile easily, I considered her tight smirk as indicating the sort of reaction another person would convey with a roar. And, I understood that she was still a little stressed about the approaching judgment.

"It is about my father's famous Rugby school. And it shows how Father and little Tom Brown bravely took on bullying. Anyhow, in the end, the bad people get expelled. And, I hope that the good people don't get expelled this time. But, regardless, remember, I've seen this sort of situation before and I'll be by your side."

"Yeah, that's working great so far." Marguerite rolled her eyes with a muted smirk. She was trying to be fun in my vein. I appreciated that. But, I could see that she was overwhelmed with worry – the turbulence of youth.

"Don't worry about the consequences of your early schooling. I was such a poor student that my best friend Clough and others organized study parties for me. They were sad to report that I went fishing all the while. The results were scandalously poor."

"You're a very strange guide."

"Dastardly. But remember, school often has very little to do with education. Education is the most precious attainment a thinking being can have. And, if you get kicked out, not being here will not slow down your education, if you will it. You'll have more time to read biographies about your wonderful Mr. Arnold."

I displayed my satisfied head on a V I made with my palms. At that Marguerite actually made a sound resembling a chortle. I was glad to make her laugh. After my exuberance got her in trouble, her giggle reassured me that I might not be such a terrible influence after all.

Principal Cross' office had a heavy dark-brown door. The door's sole small vertical rectangular window's glass had many angles designed to obscure vision. What a queer metaphor, I thought. Her office conveyed all of the heaviness of the all-too-serious Puritans. And, as with them, it had no hint of sweetness and light.

"You're not succeeding here Ms. Buckby." Principal Cross' first ominous words aimed at suffocation.

From my vantage point, Ms. Cross' statement rang true. But, with no ambitious academic liberal arts curriculum and no true teachers, how could a student like Marguerite 'succeed' at this school? I turned to Marguerite and winked to remind her of the element of play in this dramatic moment.

"In short, I am going to recommend on-line schooling for you."

"What? I am not a bad person! This can't be happening to me. I know I seem like a bad person to you. But I'm not." Marguerite shot me a dirty look as I gave her two thumbs up and smiled. I thought that as an elder male, this reassurance would help. But Marguerite was seriously committed to this drama – my gesture was decidedly not funny.

"I'm afraid, Ms. Buckby, that there are limits. We run an institution here and that requires some conformity. You seem to wish to be free. Well, you have gotten your wish."

"My father's going to kill me."

"You should have thought of that before you mocked Mr. Early."

Marguerite held her head down, and I in turn did my utmost to look as if I were at a funeral. I am glad that when Marguerite glanced at me she didn't look carefully. I could barely keep from bursting out laughing. Just below the mourning, a minor celebration was ready to erupt. We endured in silence as we waited for the paperwork. Though this process passed in moments for me, I think it seemed eternal to my young charge.

As we left Principal Cross' office, Marguerite's shrunken, curved posture had returned. Her eyes were fixed on her dragging feet.

"Watch it bitch!" A horrid young man she bumped into snarled.

"Sorry."

"Sorry!" I exclaimed, "My Dearest Heart, you shouldn't put up with such intentionally vulgar rudeness."

"He wasn't rude, that's just how people talk now days."
"Really? Love, it is not the way people have always spoken. And it is not the way all people speak. I, for one, am glad you're getting out of this vile institution. I will teach you. And, I will never degrade you with nasty language."

"But you might disappear at any time."

"Then you'd better take advantage of me while you can." I smiled wickedly.

CHAPTER
~ 9 ~

MARGUERITE'S PLAN

Marguerite nearly hurt herself as she ran to hug me and hit the wall instead. We both laughed as she regained her balance and brushed the hair out of her eyes.

"I'm back! I'm back Dear. This is delightful. How much time has elapsed since I last saw you?" I queried enthusiastically.

"It's still the same day."

"And we're in your bedroom?"

"How did you know?"

I shivered as I pointed and shot a haughty look of disapproval in the direction of a photo of Ricky wedged in her mirror frame.

"Tear it in half and put it in the rubbish bin or I won't ever speak to you ever again, ever."

"Okay, okay."

"This sort of person is a symptom of social ills you should combat, rather than stoop to. With that, you debase love!" I said standing erectly and still sternly pointing at the horrid likeness.

"Okay, okay, the photo is torn up. It's in the trash. Okay?" Marguerite protested with annoyance.

I was relieved; I did not wish to back my way out of my 'never speaking to you again' bluff. And, moreover, I was delighted to be back so soon. The posture of irritation couldn't hold much longer. I couldn't believe I returned simply on her summons. Something was afoot; this was not normal protocol. But for whatever reason, I was back and overjoyed to be so.

"I didn't call on you for boyfriend advice anyhow." The snotty little brat uttered. "Because of you, I am in trouble." The brat was on a roll! "My Dad and his girlfriend, Scamantha, will be back home soon. You have to tell me what to do." As Marguerite didn't yet seem to have vented all her rehearsed bratty comments, I let her continue.

"But, even more importantly, I've made a big decision. I want to go visit my adopted mom, Cindy and my biological mom, Twinkie."

"Twinkie?" I simply had to interject.

"Twinkie. Her real name is Carla Jean, Carla Jean Kracik."

"Okay." I said batting my eyes incredulously, "When did you decide this?"

"On my way home. I mean, I have been in contact with my biological mother for about nine months. And, I've been worried about my adopted mother, who I call 'Mom,' for a while. And, seeing them has been an impossible dream, not even worth thinking about, till now. But by getting kicked out of school, thanks to you, I am free. I can do on-line schooling, so I can do schoolwork as I travel. I already know how to drive. It's perfect. It's what I want to do."

"Well, it sounds perfect. But, what advise might I, your humble guide, provide? Tutoring services and . . ."

"Well, I don't think that Daddy will be in the mood to let me go on a trip. He'll want to punish me for getting thrown out of school. I don't think he'll want to give me a reward and let me borrow his car either. So, you're a writer, what should I tell him?"

To best advise her, I asked Marguerite to tell me more about her relationship with her adopted mother, Cindy, her 'Mom.'

Since she was about thirteen, Marguerite had tried to call her mother at least once a week. And, about every two months or so, they'd have a pretty good little talk. Her 'Mom' had a wicked sense of humor, not totally unlike mine, she said. She called her 'Mom,' because, they lived together, for eight years. And, the woman had been a mother figure, in some capacity, all of Marguerite's young life.

But, starting just under two years ago, as soon as her mother heard her voice, she'd hang up. And, Les, her mother's 'boyfriend,' (a word that didn't fit a grown man), wouldn't pass his cell phone to her. And, then he wouldn't answer his phone either. Finally, Marguerite pretty much stopped trying. Every few months she'd try. But, her mother's phone was disconnected and Dr. Les wouldn't answer.

Marguerite took the lack of phone calls personally. She had tried to be a dutiful daughter. She had called pretty regularly. And, she didn't run away from her mother; Her father had made her leave. She wanted to see what was going on, to help her mother. Face-to-face, her mother couldn't hang up. There'd probably be a fight. But, at least there'd be some communication.

Marguerite held out even more hope for the meeting with her biological mother. She had traced Twinkie down fairly easily after she found the adoption paperwork in the filing cabinet part of her father's desk. This biological mother had given birth to her at the age of fourteen.

My young orphan hoped that with a visit, she might also be able to find out who her biological father was. Then she'd be able to track him down as well. Also, she felt that by seeing her real parents, she'd come to better understand who she herself was as a person.

Marguerite had spoken with her biological mother twice. And the big news there, Marguerite conveyed with excitement, was that Marguerite had some siblings. She had already established facebook contact with one: a half-sister, named Christina.

But, her biological family was poor. They lived in Ohio and they couldn't afford to come to Los Angeles. And, Marguerite hadn't been able to visit either mother because of school. I solved that problem! I silently wondered if undertaking this sojourn might not be the very reason the powers had let me linger with Marguerite for so long.

I also sensed something terribly wrong with Marguerite's adopted mother, Cindy. Why would she so obstinately refuse to speak with this lovely, needy, girl? It seemed pathologically cold. I didn't believe Marguerite's depiction of her lovely phone relationship with 'Mom' prior to the current break in communication either. Jack had moved his daughter to Detroit and Los Angeles to get away from Cindy's problems with addiction. This didn't smell good.

"Have you mentioned visiting your mother to your father before?"

"Yeah. When I ask, he gets quiet and says, 'No.' If I mention it again, he gets really depressed. Then he gets sad for days. And, the last time I mentioned it, Oh My Gawd, he actually got angry – well as angry as Daddy can get. So, I stopped asking. That was about a year ago."

"Well, if you mention going to see Twinkie, he will know that you'll try to visit Cindy as well. By the way, I hate both their names, they sound like children's names. I also don't like when people call their parents 'Daddy' and 'Mommy,' 'Mother,' and 'Father,' are better. Your parents are adults, not children. At some level your whole nation has become infantilized."

"Okay. But, what should I do when they ask if I'm going to visit Cin – my mother?"

"I also want to say that this situation wouldn't be necessary if your society weren't so degenerate. You have no idea what a tragedy your family is for your society. I mean, of course, I feel badly for you personally, but, your national character . . . "
"Okay, okay, that's enough lecture, what should I doooo?" Marguerite whined. I stifled my desire to tell her how obnoxious her whining sounded.

"Well, you know that I am a terrible guide, right Love?"

"Yes." She smiled coyly, "But anyhow, I want your advice. So tell me what to do and I'll do it."

"I don't think your father will agree if you resolutely tell him that you want to visit this Cindy woman in addition to your newly-found biological mother. But he might allow you if you promise not to visit your adopted mother."

"So lie!" Marguerite jumped in, excited.

"Dear," I shot her a pained look, "No matter what you say, he'll know you plan to visit Cindy. It is very obvious. They live in the same state. Your denying it will allow him to the ability to deny the obvious to himself, give him room to feel he has done his best to protect you," I reasoned sympathetically. "But part of him understands that you need to see your adopted mother, it is unreasonable to keep you from her.

"God help me, I am a bad guide. But, my father, as Headmaster, as Principal, in order to instill honor, used to tell his students, 'As I trust and honor you, know that I'll believe whatever you tell me. But don't betray my trust, never lie to me.' Many times he had to know when to let a not-too-dangerous fib pass for the greater good."

I didn't feel that Marguerite was buying this type of logic, so I switched tactics. "I think I am still around because this trip is destined to happen, Sweetness. And, it feels as if it is my role, my duty, to tell you how to make it come to pass. And I think in stating that you're not going to visit your adopted mother, you will allow your father to allow you to take this journey."

"And please, Love," I said, returning to a tone of stern righteousness, "Call your Daddy, 'Father,' from now on. It will be a small concession to the moral order and help mitigate my foul sin of telling you to not be entirely forthright with him. And, furthermore, it will save me from wanting to vomit. 'Daddy!'"

To be sure, I was being dramatic. But the wreck of American life, the situations young Marguerite had to live through, truly pained me. I worried about the fate of England and the other European nations. Perhaps having a blunt look at reality was the tonic she required.

Here, in full bloom, in Marguerite's life, we saw the destructive legacy of Romantic poets, such as the licentious Byron, on Christendom. The philosophy wherein chaos creates drama and that makes for a rich soul, had always rubbed me the wrong way – cheap tricks masquerading as profound truths. You cannot have a society based on impulsive whims. Conduct, - I said to myself with a somber pause and a repeat for emphasis - conduct is the key to civilization.

But beneath my stoic posture, this painful situation struck me so that I could feel it in my lower abdomen. I wished that the wreckage of Marguerite's early life didn't necessitate such a harrowing journey. But, I now considered this direction our destiny. The powers-that-be must have let me linger in this world because they foresaw that Marguerite had to face her past in order to be kept permanently safe from suicide.

CHAPTER

~ 10 ~

FAMILY DYNAMICS

At dinner I got to meet Marguerite's father, Jack Buckby, and his girlfriend, Samantha. Jack looked breezy in his collared plaid shirt and blue sweater. He sported a jaw line strip of facial hair and groomed the rest of his just-too-long hair immaculately. He had been playing a part of the clean Midwest transplant for some time now. Under his easy manner, I could sense his fatigue. He worked very hard to be what others wished him to be.

Marguerite had described Samantha, her potential stepmother, as untrustworthy. Samantha wanted her father for his financial support and she only considered herself in every action she took. I was told to notice this tendency in 'Scammy, Scamantha.'

Samantha's face was, perhaps, too beautiful to trust. Like Jack, she had cultivated a natural look that relied on precision. Her perfectly placed lip-gloss, for example, exaggerated her authentic lip color without appearing unnatural. Likewise, I could not tell if her dirty blond hair had been dyed or not. A hint of mascara and eyebrow pencil completed the mask. She was Jack's perfectly breezy counterpart.

I personally aspire to as much beauty as my poor physical inheritance will allow. But in this I am without hypocrisy. I have never sought to be natural; I wish to excel nature. This makes me a part of the human order - above the natural order.

Whereas I researched and carefully polished my pose, and consciously chose the face I showed the world, most take their clothes and grooming cues from society without reflection. I am sure that others in Jack and Samantha's surroundings also had their studied faux naturalness.

In the absence of a true first impression of Samantha, I decided to trust her. Had I been alive, I would have been wary, but charmed her with sweetness and light. As it was, I was dead, and so confined to the sidelines.

As with all homes, the most delightful member of the Buckby household was their dog. 'Rusty,' was a playful young short-haired labrador. He and I hit it off immediately. A naturally serious dog, this boy needed love and I was happy, happy, happy, to oblige. Unfortunately, however, the seriousness of the conversation at hand required my immediate attention.

"So Maggie you've finally done it!" Her father angrily transitioned from niceties of setting up dinner to the business at hand.

"Father, it's for the best. The people at my school were vulgar."

"'Vulgar?,' 'Father?' What's gotten into you?"

"Father," I said, synching with her, "is a term of respect. It signifies that you have greater wisdom and therefore authority than I. It establishes order in society. It is more appropriate than 'Dad,' or, God-forbid, 'Daddy.'" Since I ordered this vocabulary improvement, I felt it only right that I guide her statement about it.

"Well you could have shown some respect to Mr. Early. Principal Cross said you were very rude to him."

"Respect is not only conferred due to status, it must be earned. While professing to teach, Mr. Early, in fact, is entirely uninterested in cultivation. He doesn't play his part well. He spends his days dulling young minds. He is the problem with . . ."

"You know, Maggie," her father cut us off, "I really don't want to hear it now. Mr. Early is your teacher. You have to respect him. He gives you grades. And, by failing his class . . ."

Then Jack interrupted himself, "What's happened to you? We have a nice home. I am finally with a woman who makes me happy." And at that Jack reassuringly put his hand on Samantha's knee and turned to smile at her.

Marguerite nearly rolled her eyes at this. But as she was working on conduct, she really tried to listen. She took her father seriously as he said, "You're the only piece of my world that isn't right. I am worried about you because I love you." Though he had said this often, this might have been the first time she really listened to him. Showing proper deference, instead of rolling one's eyes all the time, works social wonders.

Subtly, Jack noticed the shift in her when she listened. He picked up on the fact that she wasn't rolling her eyes. And, because his concerns had been heard, he momentarily trusted her. It took him off guard and allowed him to go farther. Changing tones entirely, Jack asked, "Have I done something wrong?"

"No Father, I love you, very much." Marguerite said quietly and with eye contact. "You haven't done anything wrong." Jack didn't acknowledge these words, but he felt them deeply. For the first time, she wasn't just blowing him off. And she wasn't just buttering him up. Marguerite had changed. "It's just that, well, high school is horrible. I hate everyone, their nastiness, their pettiness."

Then Marguerite softened her tone even further and spoke with jarring directness, "Father, I have a proposition."

"What?" Jack tensed up instinctively, knowing what was coming.

"For my part, I promise to do all of my on-line assignments by myself and do them well. And, I promise to approach my work with diligence. You won't have any worries from me. And, you know I am behind in credits? I promise I will finish my high school program ahead of schedule."

"Oh no. I know what's coming. You want to go visit your biological family and Cindy Rose, don't you?"

"It will only take me a couple of weeks. I'll get A's on all my schoolwork. I promise. Look at my grades for a while.

If I don't start well, I won't go and you won't hear a peep from me. You'll come to see you can trust me."

"No!"

"Why not?"

"Because I don't want you to visit Cindy Rose." At the mention of her, Jack began bobbing his head in a low roll, like a shamed dog. This gesture came from deep in his gut. On second thought, it reminded me more of a beaten dog, in that such dogs are continually always already anticipating abuse.

It was then that I first got a hint as to what kind of family reunion we would be sailing towards. Jack must have suffered some terrible abuse at the hands of his ex-wife.

"I won't visit Cindy Rose then. I swear. I haven't spoken to her in years anyhow. I won't visit her. I promise." Is it charming that people lie so easily? "But, I want to see my half-brothers and half-sister and my birth mother."

At this point, Samantha put her hand in Jack's hair and nearly whispered, "Jack, Baby, maybe it would be a good idea." Subtly, she turned and winked at Marguerite and continued, "I told you that Maggie has been having trouble ever since she found her birth mother online."

Marguerite nearly screamed that this was also the same time that Scamantha moved in. Inside herself, she had screamed this thought many times. But, with her target in mind, and a pinch of conduct, Marguerite remained poised. She knew that Samantha had manipulating skills she didn't have.

Samantha moved her hand down to Jack's shoulder and gently continued, "Marguerite is nearly eighteen. She is getting old enough to make her own decisions and take care of herself. We're seeing her come into her own." Touching his chin, she tried to move Jack's head to show Marguerite's reassuring nodding. But he wouldn't look. I couldn't believe she'd literally manipulate him like that.

"Besides," Samantha leaned into Jack's personal space and nearly grazed his ear with her lips, "perhaps we'll go up to the Carpenteria house at the same time, spend a little quality time together by the beach alone – just you and I." Samantha clearly saw Marguerite as an impediment to her potential spouse's affection. She didn't even try to hide it.

Then turning to Marguerite, Samantha barked, "But that can only happen if you kick ass on your homework young lady!" The smile accompanying this mock seriousness fully uncovered her manipulation skills. I didn't believe she had any concern for Marguerite's education. She wanted a vacation and time with Jack.

Jack searched for a way to forestall the inevitable rendezvous with Cindy Rose. "Well, how about you fly? That would be so much more convenient. I'll get you a plane ticket to your biological mother's city."

Samantha smiled to Marguerite as if to say, 'Don't worry kid, I can handle him.' She then she moved her eyes directly in front of Jack's. Their noses nearly touched as she said, "Dearest, you know how exciting going on a road trip is. I remember my first road trip. We partied like . . . well the point is, I think Maggie would really learn a lot from the experience."

"Father, I would. And, I promise that this trip is only for me to see my biological mother. It doesn't mean I care any less for you, but I want to meet my biological family. And I *will* meet them some day. I think it would do me a world of good to meet them now. I'll do my homework. I'll take care of my responsibilities."

Jack slumped. But Samantha lifted his head by holding it at the temple on each side. She challenged his cowed eyes to meet hers. When they did, she earnestly nodded. And, she softly used her hands on his temples to make his head nod in synch with hers.

This was how she got him to do whatever she wanted, I reasoned. It was an insidious and confrontational manipulation. But, this time it didn't work. His head just hung, languishing in her hands. His eyes sank to looking below her chin.

Then, at last, he caved in, "Okay, alright."

At that sound Marguerite shrieked like an American Indian on the warpath, "Thank you Daddy, thank you thank you, thank you." And she kept saying this as she bounced up and down and hugged him.

Though working to nod, his head still seemed unnaturally drawn to his chest. He smiled a little at being hugged. But he could not ascent to this journey with eye contact. His body still refused, was still doubled over in pain at the prospect. This pain persisted, even as the crowd was elated at its victory. And, for once, the crowd winning might have been a good thing.

CHAPTER

~ 11 ~

EDUCATION

The very next day, Marguerite and I began our cramming sessions. We met daily in the public library. Many people would find this a dull setting for a chapter. But, you, my Elevated Reader, (and if you have made it this far you most certainly qualify as one), probably agree with me that no other setting could provide a chapter with as much potential for adventure!

"My heavens, my Dear Kind Darling, thank you for this!" I exclaimed.

"You're welcome," Marguerite shrugged from a slouched position.

"No, no, no, this will not do." I insisted.

"Hrmn?"

EDUCATION

"Marguerite, Darling Dear, you have got to become clear on something about yourself."

"Such as . . ."

"You need to know that you have a life of the mind, an interior mental life, and you should be thrilled about it."

She stared at me blankly.

"Look, don't play dumb with me or I'll disappear." I humorously turned my back and shuddered as a sign of indifferent umbrage. Looking back over my shoulder, I saw Marguerite smile. "Yes, that's the spirit."

"No, you're the spirit." Marguerite laughed.

"Sharp!" I replied. "Do you know what my last words in my final report on education were?"

"No, but I have a feeling I'm going to."

I smiled as if to say 'touché.' My little charge had her sassy setting on. "My final words of my thirty-five year career were, 'Of education, information itself is really the least part.'"

"Meaning?" Her nonchalance at the momentous nature of these remarks, made me temporarily question my love for her. It passed immediately. But, she was being stubborn for no reason.

"Meaning a couple of things." I resumed with a smile, "One is that we must love learning, take a joy in learning, as a philosophy, as a mindset. Your sullen attitude towards

learning is very much of your time. It is a caked on shell, a cocoon, a snake skin, from which you must emerge."
"Wait, but you were a school inspector, right and you didn't enjoy that."

"Oh dread, a girl armed. Such a terrible thing." I smirked appreciatively while attempting to muss her hair. Unfortunately, my hand went right through her head. Reaching out to touch someone and going through them always jarred me; you feel nothing, so much nothing that you shiver, cold - a vivid reminder that you're dead.

I looked at my hand and made a slightly frustrated garumph. Marguerite, turned her head and looked at me sadly.

"We'll have none of that." I smiled. "Yes, I was a school inspector, I went from school to school inspecting the little scholars. And, yes, I often had a bad attitude. I called it drudgery and frequently complained. For thirty-five years I dragged myself from school to school, county to county, checking to see if the little monsters had been taught. Even in Winter. Can you imagine?"

"So you weren't always gay?" Marguerite smiled at the implication. She really was on the edge.

"No, I was quite somber at times. But, externally, I was gay - and, not in the way that you mean it, Beasty. Even while dreading my day job, I cut quite a figure in my long waistcoats and long hair. To be fine, to be elegant, it is a thing that gets at the very heart of life. Conduct is key.

"And, this is not just, as you say, 'covering up.' Perhaps I cannot convey this to you adequately, but it is your duty to have fun. It is rude to sulk in the face of death. To go into your studies with the idea that this is something you'd rather not do, is the wrong approach. I want you to work on taking pride in your elegance, the fact that you're a thinking being. Enjoy your cultivation, your mind."

"Well, alright Daaaaahling!" She gestured with a flip of the wrist.

"Yes, I have always called everyone 'Darling,' men, women, everyone. It is one of my best extravagances. It is lovely and it wakes people up. It lends oneself to what I call 'sweetness and light.' Can you hear the ostentatious tone of the phrase, 'sweetness and light'?"

"Yes. It feels quite elegant Daaaaahling." She smiled, miming taking puff on a long cigarette holder with her other hand by her head.

"Yes. But, this edifice cannot be built on air. True haughtiness, requires we've something to be haughty about. We must be large of mind, expanded through study. We must understand the best that has been thought and said in the world. We must walk through life as a general, overlooking the entire battlefield of time, not simply muddle through in the miserable confines, situations and cultural assumptions of our years.

"Look at this library, Marguerite. In each of these books, we have a chance to converse with great minds and visit wonderful epochs. We can, in short," I announced with a dramatic sweep of my arms, "play like Gods!"

At that Marguerite swung her arms wide and yelled, "Play like Gods." And, just like that, it happened. As she spoke psychically, the arms of her spirit body swung free from her 'real' body. She stood up and looked back at her sunken self and poor posture.

"Shall we dance?" I asked. We both danced about the library, in a drunken waltz, until doubled over in laughter. Her imagined body went through tables gracefully. This amazed me. I had never, ever, ever had such an experience with a person I had been sent to guide before. I was overwhelmed by the fun.

"You're quite the dancer." Marguerite exclaimed.

"You, Dearest Love, are not bad yourself. I am so very, very, very happy to have had this dance with you." I bowed with glee, eliciting a curtsy from my dance partner.

Given a moment to catch a breath's absence, I reflected on the fact that I had never in my previous century – plus as a guide, been with anyone for more than half an hour. I never even knew it was possible for a living person to gain metaphysical powers such as Marguerite just displayed. Why was this happening? I wondered. Then seeing Marguerite standing and smiling, I remembered the task at hand.

"Okay now, Darling Dearest, to study. And no frowning." She returned to her body and sat upright.

"Well, first I have a question, Mr. Arnold."

"A question, most excellent!"

"But it's about you."

"That is not so interesting. I told you about my not wanting a biography, didn't I?"

"Yes, but we're friends, aren't we?"

"Very much so My Close Love."

"So, Ian Hamilton's book, which I have been reading, says that when you got married, it sort of ended your life; that you were a very great poet and you threw it all in the trash for marriage. Why did you do it?"

"Well Mr. Hamilton thinks fairly highly of himself and is rather dismissive of me. I wrote poems all my life, even up through the year I died. Okay, I'll admit that they lacked the freshness and inspiration of my earlier productions. But I also wrote massively in prose. I was quite productive."

Marguerite looked unconvinced.

"I wrote more on education than any other Victorian." I insisted. "I was a leading religious writer and launched the field of Celtic studies. I was my Victorian era's most quoted social critic. I launched literary criticism! I would like to see Mr. Hamilton match that output, work a full-time job and still find time to write greater poetry than I did!"

My temper back in possession, I put my left and right fingertips together and smiled, reassuringly. "On the matter of my stepping away from poetry in favor of a real job and prose, Lionel Trilling's biography of me comes much closer to the truth than Hamilton's does. Have you read him?"

"Nope."

"Please do. It will be a milestone. He is quite the intellectual biographer."

"So, what did Trilling say? Why did you throw poetry away for marriage?" I could feel Marguerite's disapproval of this decision.

"Well, My Dearest Heart, it is true, I did sacrifice a lot to marry my Darling Incomparable Flu. Prior to my marriage, and the diminution of my poetic powers, prior to my thirty-five years as a school inspector, I worked for, (and when I say 'worked for' I mean 'occasionally translated a letter for'), Henry Petty-Fitzmaurice, the Third Marquis of Lansdowne."

"That is quite a name." She audibly laughed, holding her fingers to her nose to silence the sound.

"He was quite the man, My Man. Educated, refined. He was the last of the pretentious aristocrats. He became a bit of an ideal for me."

"Imagine!" Marguerite said wistfully, referring to her burgeoning understanding of my appreciation.

"And 'My Man Lansdowne,' as I called him, gave me entre to the best circles in London and the most up-to-date information. It was during this time that my dandy ways peaked. In addition to my old Oxford classmates, I scandalized all the best people of London.

"After marriage, I kept up my image as best I could. But, poverty, decades of drudgery, and a family, took a toll on my clothes and, yes, occasionally, my exuberance."

"It sounds like you were pretty happy 'working' for Lansdowne," Marguerite offered to bring my spirits back up.

"Oh yes! Beauty surrounded me and I had time. Time is so important." I said, pausing for emphasis, "And, My Man Lansdowne appreciated my time. As a man of cultivation himself, he understood the importance of my literary pursuits. He let me spend long hours in the Athenaeum club, named after Athena, the goddess of wisdom, don't you know; a meeting place and great library for people who live in the life of the mind.

"So working for My Man Lansdowne, I could indulge my mind and write poem after poem concerning the role of a poet. It is an important, if idle, topic with which to play. In fact, at a time, I found the role of the poet all the more wonderful because he is idle in this purpose-driven mechanical world."

"It sounds so ideal Daaaahling. I am glad you came back to me looking like you did then, in your dandy prime, quite the freak!" Being as I looked forty, I took that as a compliment rather than an oversight. Marguerite beamed. Then bringing the dandy play down a notch she earnestly pleaded, "I am still angry that you threw it all away. Again, why'd you do it, my Lovely Darling Dearest?"

"In youth, Dear Young Charge, one might painfully dig into the depth of the soul. It is a necessary training for the artist. But, if you do so, you'll find, as my creation Empedocles did, . . ."

"That poem is too long!" Marguerite honestly, but impetuously, interrupted me. If her increasing rudeness, her sassiness, was a symptom of her growing into her own,

I wasn't sure I wanted to see it. In order to express my growing annoyance over her bratty nature, I rolled my eyes, straightened my arms as if to look at the back of my hands from a distance, took my smile down a notch, and feigned a heavy sigh.

"Thank you Dear, as I was saying," Marguerite, endearingly, paid rapt attention to express her remorse over her prior rudeness, "Empedocles was the ultimate in self-absorbed romantic exploration. He couldn't reconcile himself to the fact that his lovely ephemeral thoughts lived in a material world. Identifying with his thoughts, he felt he didn't belong among all this . . . stuff. And so I wrote:

But, mind, but thought –

If these have been the master part of us –

Where will they find their parent element?

What will receive them, who will call them home?

But we shall still be in them, and they in us,

And we shall be the strangers of the world,

And they will be our lords, as they are now:

And Empedocles found his thoughts frustratingly small and confining. He complained that our thoughts:

"keep us prisoner of our consciousness,

And never let us clasp and feel the All

But through their forms, and modes, and stifling veils.

EDUCATION

And we shall be unsatisfied as now;
And we shall feel the agony of thirst,
The ineffable longing for the life of life
Baffled for ever; and still thought and mind."

"I'm sorry, Darling, was that too long for your impatient mind?" I snidely asked.

"No, when you explain it, as a restless mind looking for a place on this earth, with no home, and frustrated by how small our thoughts are; calling us 'prisoners of our consciousness,' I get it. It's so cool."

"Please remember, though, the poem represents the overblown rhetoric of a self-absorbed romantic. The Romantics – like me, in my youth – to a certain extent – withdrew into ourselves. We searched for depth and reality in our own souls - and only in our own souls. Then, finding no satisfaction there, the Romantics ran out to have intense experiences – sexual trysts and battles in the world of action."

"Yes. I love that! I want intense experiences." Marguerite beamed.

"But these people remained outsiders."

"Yes, passionate outsiders. So beautiful." She unconsciously approved.

"Lovely Dear. Yes, your shallow society still worships a faded distant echo of the Romantic Era. And you swallow it without reflection. It is pathetic."
"What!"

"Well, yes. 'Kicks,' remains the advertised goal of your nation; The search for something exciting, something outside of society. No? Your musical entertainers all dress as if they've been through a tornado. But. they haven't. They are faded echoes of the Romantics; without Empedocles' intellectual struggles prior to their pose of glory, with no semblance of philosophy. Your society's advertised goals are, I am sorry to say, sad, hollow, pathetic faded echoes of the Romantic's, kicks; anti-social and anti-intellectual."

Sensing that my young charge was getting something out of what I had just said, I braved another illustration, "This reminds me of another poem of mine. Can I briefly tell you about it?"

"Sure," Marguerite murmured, suddenly taken aback by the fact that Matthew Arnold was really in front of her. Then seeing my expression she snapped back to reality and brightly chirped, "Of course!" Conduct covered my momentary dread.

"My poem 'Mycerinus,' portrays a just and virtuous king, Mycerinus, who is told he has only six years to live. His father was an evil ruler and he lived to a very old age. His likewise evil grandfather also lived into old age. But young Mycerinus, who was a very responsible and good King, was told he only had six years to live. He had been fated to die young."

"Oh. I see. That's not fair."

"Precisely."

"What does he do, the king?" She asked.

"Mycerinus pulls out of society and 'parties,' to use your vernacular, until he dies. He becomes a Dionysian reveler, a partier, out of rage, out of anger over the world not being fair."

"Oh. I could see doing that. What is the point of being good when it doesn't get rewarded? What's the point of working when you're just going to die? We might as well just party." She calmly reasoned.

"Yes. But, Mycerinus' country would have been much better off if he conscientiously continued his rule for his final years, rather than party in a tantrum because life was unfair. There would have been more dignity in it. We all die. But, life matters.

"And so too I, when I got married, decided to give up self-centered, self-indulgent romantic poetry for responsible engagement with the world."

"Ah, like the king should have."

"Yes, and as Empedocles should have, My Love. And, of course, when I got married and took a job, a real job, the romantic inspired, wild part of me shrank. And, my poetry suffered." At this, my dear Marguerite looked anguished.

"That's a shame."

"Well perhaps poetically. But that's what marrying My Incomparable Essential Flu required. Her father, a Judge, had money and I was an impoverished dandy. He, rightfully, wouldn't allow his daughter to marry me unless I had a real job."

"Horrible," she shuddered, "A real job."

"See? That is the very reaction, I fought against. I understand it. Believe me, drudgery taught me about the drudgery of drudgery being drudgery!" At that I rolled my eyes up for the silliness of language, and Marguerite smiled.

"But, I could not be the poet who removes himself forever to search his supposedly profound soul – like Empedocles, or just party like Mycerinus.

"I chose to enter the world on its own terms. Getting married and having children and committing to their support provided a framework for that. It led me to turn my intellect to the public's consciousness, to securing a healthy culture for my offspring to be raised in. In short, I left adolescence and grew up."

Haughtily, I placed my hand in front of sternum and elevated my chin. Then, pushing my hands forward in protest, I concluded, "For this, some critics have never forgiven me. And this says more about them, the critics, and more about their culture than it says about me. They haven't grown up."

"I see. That makes sense. But, wasn't there some feeling of loss?"

She would not let it rest. But, I answered with honesty and decorum, "Oh yes, I still ask, as I did in my poem, 'Youth and Calm:'

'And when this boon rewards the dead,

Are all debts paid, has all been said?'

"The worry that I may have made the wrong choice still occasionally haunts me." I quipped with emphasis and a smile for my ironic use of the word 'haunt.' "But, I am thrilled with my output." She still looked unimpressed.

Hitting at the hard shell of her dismissals, I continued, "Flu's father was right! To be a proper man for my Incomparable Essential Flu, a proper father, I needed the stability of a home – not turmoil and endless parties. To continue to flitter and revel would have been like Empedocles isolated with his thoughts. To be a real person, I needed to be a part of this world. And only from this vantage point could I really be a proper critic, don't you see?"

I could feel my ire rising with her continued disapproval. "And, yes, if in the bargain I lost some of my ability to write profound poetry, well that's just too bad."

And, I climaxed in the very tone of my scolding father. "But, to not grow up is pathetic – I didn't want to end up like Byron and Shelly (from whom we learned nothing), dead, ruined and disgraced. As my best biographer, Trilling, noted, it was a conscious calculated sacrifice. I rarely regret it."

"Hmmn," Marguerite groaned, not totally convinced.

"It is not sad at all." I said confidently, "Empedocles, the poem, was, as you said, too long. The man was deep, but far too self-involved. His going on and on and on about the place of thought in the world was nauseating. And, the ending provides the proof."

"I'm sorry. I suck. I never made it to the end."

"Suicide! Suicide! In despair of ever totally feeling the universe, Empedocles kills himself by jumping into a volcano."

"Oh my God."

"Yes!" I exclaimed, knowing that I was treading on a delicate subject, somewhat nervously, I changed subjects and lowered my tone. "I had a poem called 'Resignation,' in which I pleaded,

'Blame thou not, therefore, him who dares

Judge vain beforehand human cares;'

"I asked the reader to not blame the escapist poet. But, I do blame him. I blame him for the rotten, self-indulgent, anti-social, romantic, shallow nature of your culture. And, truth be told, even for your following in Empedocles' suicidal foot-steps."

She seemed to have eaten a bit of her heart at this statement. And, I saw that I was, too, letting my emotions get the better of me.

"It's natural." I calmly nodded and concluded, "A passionate inquiry into the nature of the soul and brooding is natural to youth – it was what was trendy in my day too. But looking outside of myself, I could see that my dear England was in danger and needed my attention, so I quit brooding and got serious."

"In danger of what?" She asked innocently.

"In danger of falling into a spiritual and intellectual abyss, endangered by crass materialism."

"Oh my God," Marguerite said, "You actually remained a Romantic after all, huh?"

"To a great extent. Yes, My Darling, to a great extent. And, as a core Romantic, I, at first, resented my job. But, when I finally accepted my position as school inspector, I realized remaking the culture by remaking education could be a valiant mission; It became a passion for me. When I accepted my role in society, I had a great spiritual rebirth from a poet to a social critic."

"And, did many people listen to you. Did your switch to helping society work?"
"A bit." I reported. "I hope my work steered British culture towards appreciating the mind and aiming their thoughts at the perfect social world." And at that, reflecting on the irrelevance of my output, I felt a bit sad. I felt as if my marriage, my leaving poetry, was a bad choice, like I had exchanged my soul to gain the world and lost both.

"Well don't be down, Mr. Arnold." Marguerite offered –in a reverse of roles, cheering me up. "I cannot blame him who dares, one who dares be a part of this world, one like you!"

With still sad eyes, I smiled brightly. She got my message. That had to be enough. I was deeply gratified to have a student listen to me again.

In the weeks that followed, I introduced young Marguerite to Sophocles, Goethe, Darwin, Newton and Plato. This was exquisite. Having an opportunity to educate a young mind meant having an excuse to read the classics again. To have such an opportunity, after you've already died is, - well, try to imagine it. Now I really was in heaven.

Marguerite passed all of her classes within weeks. Jack and Samantha were very happy. But, Marguerite's real achievement lay in cultivating a playful thirst for learning. My favorite thing, next to my family, was to be alone translating Greek. Marguerite learned that spending time alone, cultivating one's self, was a source of pride and beauty.

And, cutting a fine line between the romantic and pragmatic, I tried to impress upon my young charge the importance of such a learning regimen for one's nation. If one becomes their 'best self,' they have a vantage point by which to judge others. They have standards. And, thus they can teach citizens what is worthy of them and what is crass.

Learning, becoming elegant, I taught Marguerite during our weeks of library joy, is a social, as well as a personal, duty. Greek accents and physiology alone, are just isolated facts. Instrumental knowledge does not, on its own, lead to anything but being a specialist. To make knowledge useful, it must relate to our instinct for beauty, to our instinct for conduct. No civilization worth the time ever resulted from anything but its citizens understanding beauty and conduct.

'Of education,' as I had said, 'information itself is really the least part.'

CHAPTER
~ 12 ~

ROAD TRIP

Jack and Samantha saw us off. Samantha smiled widely throughout our departure. I thought it somewhat wonderful that, on an early Sunday hour of 8:30 A.M., for the intimate occasion of seeing her potential stepdaughter off, Samantha had applied her faux natural makeup perfectly.

As I got in the passenger seat of the square-roofed, four-door, brown automobile, I felt a bit unnerved. I was use to trains. But, this was only the second time I had been in an automobile. The closeness of the engine's power scared me. And, the very idea of entering such a small metal box and moving at high speeds, made me feel like an object.

Americans' relentless propensity to move, their journeying across land too much and within their psyches too little - their mania for road trips to nowhere - perfectly mirrors their interiors. I don't like car culture. I made a haughty face. The very phrase, 'car culture,' is repulsive.

"I guess." Marguerite mused.

"Oh you were listening, Love!" I chirped happy to have been heard.

"Sometimes when I am very quiet," The young colt affirmed, "I can hear your thoughts. I enjoy them. I like how you have a cheery tone, even in disdain."

"Lovely Darling Angel, you know, charm, when mixed with sweetness and light, automatically relaxes and elevates. And," I added mischievously, "allows you to attack at will! People don't know what to say if you skewer them playfully, with a smile.

 "Were I purely nasty, you wouldn't even hear me if I spoke out loud. And, as life ends quickly, we should never really entertain malice. We must be kind to each other, . . ." I paused for my punch line, "even to the vapid and wrong." I smiled broadly, enjoying my naughtiness.

Checking her reaction, mid-smile, I turned to see that Marguerite was busy speaking to her father through the car window. My young chauffer revved the engine several times as we waited to leave. At each swell, her father took a crest-fallen step backwards. She looked out the window and told Jack and Samantha she'd be safe and she'd call one last time. And we were off.

As we left, I looked back. The revving had visibly diminished her father (who already looked like he'd been punched in the stomach). But at each crescendo, potential-stepmother Samantha supplemented her waving with small lifts onto her toes. She was excited for us. She was taller for the experience. We stopped at the stop sign, looked back one last time, turned right and were gone.

"This is tremendously exciting!" I exclaimed, doing my best to hide my unease over being in a moving box.

"Yes. It is. I am so glad to be going; to be gone, from this town; and, to be going on this trip with you." Marguerite smiled one of her sheltered, yet beaming little grins at me, up through her stringy long hair; both her hands nearly higher than her head on the steering wheel.

"Did you notice your father and Samantha's different reactions to your increasing the loudness of the engine?"

"Yep. And, that's why I stopped revving the engine. I realized my excitement was hurting my father."

"That is tough, Dear. I appreciate your sensitivity, but I'd recommend against shrinking yourself to fit others' capacity for joy. If others are miserable, you needn't be." We both smiled and nodded, agreeing to be as happy as possible!

"And so, as in my poem 'Resignation,' we are going back to the land of your childhood, returning to a place you haven't been in a long time, Ohio. To look upon it once again."

"I liked that poem, 'Resignation.' That's the 'Blame thou not, him who dares' poem you mentioned. I actually understood it. It was about you and your sister visiting the same place a second time, as adults, right?"

"Yes. Hey!" I screeched.

"Sorry. I won't speed up for yellows that much again . . . or would that be shrinking to fit into other's ability to be happy?"

"You really are a devil Dear, you know that?"

"Takes one to know one." She said. Then, shifting gears, so to speak, she returned to the poem.

"So, in the poem, 'Resignation,' you compared what the hills looked like when you were kids to what they looked like when you were adults, you and your sister, right?"

"Perfect. That's it, My Heart, perfect."

"That is such a cool idea for a poem."

"I thought so!" I gleamed. And, getting to a high point of the poem, I added, "I told my dear sister, K, that being able to look over the change of time, from our first visit to our second, made us like poets, above the moment, able to survey the whole of life and compare. And that's when I suggested the ideal of the detached mystic poet daring to not care about the world, looking at it from a historically neutral, elevated, detached vantage point."

"And, your sister K didn't buy it, right?" My precocious little driver crowed at her understanding and being able to compete with me. "I mean, from what I think, we're in this incredible moment of my freedom, driving, here and now, and I don't need to compare to other moments or to some long dead ideal. I can just enjoy it – be in the moment."

"Yes, Dear, like a rock, without mind or the ability to reflect, without a history or a future – just now - a romantic rock. Sorry. But, no Dearest, I didn't leave poetry or denounce the Romantic poets to be 'in the moment.' I have always aimed for the historical perspective we get from comparing times. And, mine is a social mission. No. Detachment was not then and is not now my aim."

"No. Your goal is a-ttachment, to get maaaaaarried!" Marguerite cheered sarcastically.

"Yes." I said defensively, "To my Incomparable Lovely Essential Flu." I said defensively, "And make a difference in the world."

"Well, I can appreciate that. I like to think of myself as a bit of an activist."

"Ughh. I hate that word. What if it were a philosophy? 'I am an activist. I believe in action.' Do you see where pure activity, without thought, would just be random and stupid? It couldn't even properly be a philosophy, just movement."

"Yah, that makes sense. Perhaps I should consider becoming a thoughtivist." She smiled with a small self-satisfied grin. It was so nice that I'd been with her so long. No matter how often I implicitly judged her thoughts, I showed temper, I loved her. She felt that I loved her.

Then I shifted, "Speaking of comparing the past and present, what do you remember of your grandparents?"

"I only just have good memories of my time in Detroit with them. I remember my room in my grandparents' home. It was small. My bed felt large, but now I don't think that it was. My father would remember better than I do. It was his bedroom when he was a child."

"Oh, learning from comparison over time!" I exclaimed, glad to score one for my side.

"Yes. Score one for your side." We both smiled.

"You'd have thought my grandfather," it dawned on Marguerite, "with his management job, whatever it was, could have gotten a bigger place. But, he didn't. It was comfortable, but it was small."

"My best memory is from then is going to the Detroit museum. I mostly remember the Diego Rivera murals. They were larger and more imaginative than anything I had seen in my life. They were very serious and about workers and unions the kind of stuff that I didn't really care about. But I just saw them as huge and full of amazing color. It made me dizzy. It was amazing."

"Sublime," I interjected. As Marguerite furrowed her brows, I clarified. "A dizzy fear, that you'll be swept away, engulfed, in the rapture, in the all-consuming beauty of a piece of art."

"Yes! Sublime." Marguerite savored having learned the real meaning of the word 'sublime' as she turned the car left. "After that first time, when I went with my school, I begged my grandparents to take me back to the museum over and over. It was about an hour drive from our house. And, they took me three times. Three times. When I was younger, I was pissed that they didn't take me more. But, now, when I think about it, I think that it was loving of them to take me at all. I know they loved me.

"Oh my God. Mr. Arnold, you're crying."

"I am sorry. Ever since I died, I get moved very easily. In my life I concealed a lot of emotion. Now, I have very little control, I understand the fragility of everything – the preciousness of the moments, like you had in museum. I don't know if it was their love for you or the beauty of your connecting with the sublime in the museum or just hearing a human voice. But that is a very, very lovely memory Dearest Musette."

At that, the onramp light turned green for us, and we surged onto the number 101 freeway. Moving at a speed of nearly 76 miles an hour, Marguerite half-closed her eyes. She enjoyed the sound of the wind coming through the half cracked window. She could actually feel the ends of her hair dancing in the wind.

She whispered to herself, "I am away, finally from all of the noise, from the drama, and just here and free, in a neutral space. So, this is what it feels like to be happy!"

And, just before she noticed it, I saw the largest most expressive goofy grin on her face that I'd ever seen there. And when she noticed it, her smile extended even further. Even the sides of her eyes smiled. I was so glad that her happiness did not recede when she noticed it. Her capacity for joy was expanding.

Then I went into an odd cycle of thoughts, thoughts about thoughts. First I thought about our thoughts about traveling not being thoughts because they just reflect the actions of our moving in space. "Only thoughts about thoughts are really thoughts." I thought.

Then I thought about my thoughts taking me out of the moment and how much I love that; I love that my thoughts can take me to far away places. Then, I went back into silently looking at the freeway that stretched out before us, without thoughts. Then I returned to focusing on my thoughts again. I used my mind to toggle in and out. Perspectives.

"Yet," I summarized silently, "reflection beats resignation." In my poem, 'Resignation,' my sister and I considered how different the hills had looked during our childhood. I had asked her to look at them as a lofty poet would. Then the request was elevated as it became part of the poem 'Resignation.' And, now, one hundred years later, I was reflecting on the poem from a nearly historic perspective.

Writing allows us to accumulate and compare our thoughts over time and so to have thoughts about thoughts. When we compare two or more instances we get inner guidance, thoughtful inner guidance. This beats my charge's unconscious following of the freeway. I think.

Oscar Wilde - who introduced himself to me as a student, and spent much of his literary life countering me - claimed that the chief charm of youth was its ability to smile for no reason. While I lived, I cultivated that ability by being pleased with myself and appreciating how quickly life could end. Despite my differences with Wilde, I too had learned to smile for no reason.

Wilde even undertook a road trip of America after I did. But, he never engaged the world as a whole. He stood for art for art's sake. I reflected, criticized and engaged socially, while also aiming at promoting beauty's ways. That's why my work will prove to be of more lasting value than Wilde's.

CHAPTER
~ 13 ~

PAST, PRESENT, FUTURE

"You know," I broke in after about 30 minutes of Marguerite's savoring the road, "I was quite the traveler in my day."

"Yes. You went to America once, didn't you?"

"Ah, yes, my *two* trips to America were small disasters. This great land and I did not agree. Partially, my poor welcome in America came from perception that I criticized it harshly, which I did." I said, looking at the housing behind the chain link that lined the freeway, "But, while that was true, I threw no more attitude at America than I threw at my own nation." Being joyful and for joy, I ignored the ugliness of houses next to the freeway.

"Yes, towards the end of my life I did venture across your continent twice. But, when I think of my travels, I mostly think of my travels across Europe." We turned right on a ramp that went even higher in the sky and deposited us on the number 5 freeway.

"Oh. Like the one where you met my namesake, Marguerite?"

"Oh, yes. Beautiful. I remember my first big university-age trip across Europe, the travel that would be for me as this journey is for you, my first. On my maiden European voyage I visited *my* literary hero, George Sand."

"What was he like?"

"She," I corrected her.

"She?!" She exclaimed.

"Yes, Sweetness, George was not an uncommon women's name back then - short for Georgina, Georgia. She was very gracious. But people are never so impressive as their art is. That is even true for those of us who strive to make our lives' very moments a form of art."

"Wow. The wonder of that. The wonder of you, Mr. Arnold."

Her fawning visibly embarrassed me. As such, she mercifully mocked me, "Wow. Meeting your literary idol. It must be nice." Marguerite again smiled at me. "I hope I can meet a writer who I admire someday." She enjoyed my discomfort.

But I smiled a knowing smile and sallied forth, "Yes. We had lunch in Sand's garden." I paused, reflected and continued, "And, she was very plain, very ordinary. Her being plain was a shock because her work was so French, so scandalous. It was such a breath of fresh air to us righteous, stuffy Englishmen. She seemed to offer revolution. But, in fact, she only offered tea and cake."

"Scandalous; the woman George - interesting!" Marguerite exclaimed.

"But when I think of my travels, I mostly think of the visits I took to the continent as a school inspector; inspecting the schools of France, Holland, and Germany."

"Boring!"

"Mature! Necessary! Invigorating!" I shot back mocking her tone.

"Okay." She shot me a humorous nasty squint, while keeping her eyes on the road, "What did you learn there?"

"I learned, My Darling Sunshine, that all conversation is charming, if you fill it with play, sweetness, and light. Let's play language."

My insistence must have worked because Marguerite kicked out an "Okay, Daaarling," in imitation of me. "Hit me with the intrigue of your very lovely school inspections." Her attempt to imitate me amused me to no end. I sparkled as I looked at her. She knew how much I loved her, love being the key to all 'sweetness and light' in conversation.

"First of all," I forged on with this modicum of consent, "Nothing is separate from a critique of life. This was my motto for all of my work. That is what makes me a first rank literary critic, probably the greatest since Aristotle." And by flipping my hair with my hand, overdramatically, I pulled another smile from Marguerite. Though not discussing the topic she wanted, Sand, my mannerisms entertained her.

"Yes. To judge anything, a poem, a school system, is to promote a vision of the world. To see it from some vantage point, do you see? So when you judge a work of poetry, you implicitly spread a vision of the world."

"Well, to say what is good and bad, you need to have an opinion, I guess."

"A philosophy of life is not an opinion, My Emerging Love – the two are not the same. 'Opinion' being a very American term which is, as the Americans are, very dismissive of thought." At that I got the sourpuss look I so often evoked on my American tours. "I'm sorry Dear, the Americans are, as you say, 'The number one,' in fact, 'the very number one-est.'" I gave a sharp taut smile.

"But, in my school inspections, I came to the conclusion that my England was not very the number one-est. All the other western nations had public schools. But our nation was too proud of its individualism to have public institutions. England has long lacked a sense of collectivity. If the state made public schools, I reasoned, we could all, individually, and as a culture, strive together towards perfection, towards our best selves, as one. Public schools would elevate us, collectively."

"Public schools?" She quipped sarcastically. "Like with Mr. Early? Really?" Then without giving more thought to her rude, and perhaps deserved, dismissal of my uplift-through-public school idea, she whined, "I wanna hear more about George, pleaaaaase!"

"Okay!" I affirmed, miffed at her summary dismissal of my school plan, "But Sand was a youthful fascination; I am trying to tell you of more mature concerns."

"But, I'm still a kid." Marguerite observed, accurately enough.

As I spoke, my young driver nearly-automatically reached around to the back of the driver's seat and pulled out a bag of rancid rot with which you Americans appropriately call 'junk,' and slander culinary sensibility by associating with the word 'food.' She put the foil bag between her legs and seemed very happy. She was looking forward, with all of her attention on the road. She only listened to me as if she were listening to music. Very well.

To compare is to judge. I have a pedantic nature – I need to teach. I promised myself I would try to relax 'in the moment' with this little one and accept her for who she was – bratty nature and all. But, as a guide, I felt I had to impart information to my charge. I had decided it was the right thing to do.

"By the way, as a ghost I don't need to eat. So don't bother offering me any of your food-like substances." Unfortunately, my moralizing inclination was poisoning my conversation.

"Oh, sorry. I got kinda engrossed in the happiness of the moment." She smiled sarcastically, letting me know she was listening with a nearly imperceptible look in my direction.

"An oversight you'll correct with polite offers to the other hungry ghosts you'll meet in the future, I'm sure." I smiled conciliatorily. She smiled and looked at me out of appreciation. Then she went immediately back to chewing her chemically treated potato remnants.

"George Sand had a peculiar habit of dressing as man." I said knowing she'd find this titillating. "And, it wasn't even her real name; Her real name was Aurore. George was her male pen name."

"I knew something was up with her name. Rad."

"Meaning?"

"So bad." Then, realizing I still didn't understand, offered, "Extraordinary."

"Good, we have communicated across the ages. Speaking of which, Sand lived a long time, and so developed over time. She did not remain an adolescent all her life."

"You're a bit angry at me." Marguerite mock frowned.

"A tad, Dear Heart. But, I'll try to keep it under control."

"I am allowed to act immature." She pouted, whining with extra drama as if to drive the point home.

"You're quite right. I sincerely apologize Love. I had thought that very thought but it had not yet really sunk in with me until you said it. You're right. I apologize for judging you."

With this she let recrimination pass. People love an apology. My dear Marguerite was not without a serious side. But, as with the garbage food, I could not stand the impertinence with which she sometimes treated her own mind. Time is short. Her time with me would be short.

Time being what it might, I returned to her requested story from my youth, "My university chums and I loved Sand's boldness when she said of the artist," I quoted, "he has 'the soul of an apostle and the courage of a martyr, he has simply to push his way among the heartless and aimless crowds which vegetate without living.'"

"That sounds like you in your early romantic poet phase where you were above your boring friends, when you pushed them away too."

"Precisely. Sand fed that. And, when I was a romantic, I tried my best to be her; to be worthy of her. George Sand inspired all of us. But, I took her especially seriously. Yet I could not reconcile with her scandalous French characteristic of lubricity."

"Lubricity?"

"Her lack of commitment."

"Lack of commitment?"

"Dear, don't make me say it. You know exactly what I'm getting at. I don't wish to be lewd in front of you."

"Oh My Gaawd. You're such a prude."

"Well, I understood her reasons for denouncing marriage; 'the weakness it causes in a woman, the brutality it invites in a man,'" I said, quoting one my lines inspired by Sand.

"But, . . . ?"

"But, the French race has a very looseness which is its undoing. You take the freedom of the Gaul race, and mix it with the sensuousness of the Latin race and . . ."

"Oh My Gaawd, you're a racist too! 'Prudy the Racist!' That's your new name: Prudy the Racist! Prudy the Racist! Prudy the Racist!" She chanted, with mocking joy.
"Oh My Gaawd," I mocked back, "You're being very, very . . . too much now. You only wish to hear about fun topics and chastise me for going outside of your decade's little assumptions about right and wrong. Let's just turn on a television and watch one of your father's programs shall we?"

"But, ya are Blanche ya aaaare Prudy the Racist."

I assumed that her strange wording referred to some popular culture phenomenon. But, putting that aside, I made my rejoinder. "You shouldn't be so programmed by the wording of your own time – the assumptions of your country. The word 'education' comes from the Latin, 'educare.' It means to draw out; It aims to draw you out of your myopic little range. It makes you less likely to say, 'Oh my Gawd.'" I smiled my disarming smile that I always used when being mean. But, I knew that her culture's morality would allow her no humor in the face of the serious accusations of 'racism' and 'prudery.'

"Look, when ever you read 'race' in an old author's work, think 'culture.' The French do have a culture. Can I say that?"

"Well, yes, I guess so."

"Okay. Well these cultures impact history. For example, when the Germans – the most moral people who ever lived - embraced the Protestant Reformation, the French did not. The French could not accept the Protestant Reformation's dour seriousness."

"The Germans are the most moral people ever? What about the Holocaust? You did hear about that in heaven, didn't you?"

Trying to insert some humor, I said, "Yes I did Blanche, I did." in a tone somewhat like hers. In reply to her glum reception I uttered, "Oh Mein Gott, you've no humor around this subject. You're being a little German Furer." I chided. And, then I impulsively stuck my tongue out at her. She poked just a tiny bit of tongue tip through her mouth and bent it up to touch her lip. As good as a wink.

"When I say moral, it isn't necessarily a good thing. Seriously. I relentlessly criticized the Puritans, English and American, for being far too moral, too serious and lacking sweetness and light. Yes. The Germans are and have always been overly serious and overly moral. Is that racist? Can I say that?"

She sort of nodded.

"In fact, in my cultural analysis, in 1880, I worried about German corporalism and Kruppism. And I used those very words."

"What do those words mean?"

"They mean, My Dearest One, that I warned about the very essence of the coming fascist tide. Mussolini described 'fascism,' as 'corporatism.' That is why my noting the German propensity to corporalism was so accurate. And the Krupp corporation actually helped run fascist Germany. So I predicted fascism from my cultural analysis. So please don't tell me my ideas are verboten just because, I use the cardinal sin word of 'race' in my writing. So petty, so *your decade*." I humorously scoffed with a high flip of the wrist.

"Sorry."

"Not a problem, Love. But you must learn to think outside of your own time's prejudice a bit." Then condescendingly, but with affection, I added, "With time; Dear, with study and time.

"And, so, getting back on track," I regained the thread, "Sand, though marvelous, was too French, too promiscuous for my extremely prudish, Prudy the Prude sensibilities, and, might I add, my very Englishness."

"Well, from the American point of view, we don't care about that. Tell me why you'd be against her having several boyfriends or girlfriends or whatever she wants."

"Nations which are not moral, fall. You cannot have a drugged people dropping babies everywhere and expect the nation to do anything but decline. We're humans, not beasts." Just then I felt Marguerite move miles away. And, then I realized why. "I'm sorry, Dearest, I didn't mean to impugn your biological mother or your adopted mother." Then she smiled a sad forgiving smile that nearly broke my heart.

"It's k." She mumbled and slurred.

"At any rate, Sand's work was liberating. Is liberating. But, while it is better than the far-too-serious German literature, following her vision would ultimately bankrupt France.

"As a student, as an English student - the dullest of all the world's creatures - I found her flexible, light, wicked thought, liberating. But, in the end, Sand's failure to question her very Frenchness made her less valuable to me as I aged."

"I can see that. It is weird how you talk of nations as people. And, you criticize them like characters. It's cool. Even people, for you, represent nations and their hang-ups or whatever."

"We have to do this. It is our job as citizens, as social critics and even as artists. Humans live in culture, like it or not. That is why I wrote against just 'doing as one pleases.' I have a very social conscience."

And, as I said these words, Marguerite entered deeper into her own thoughts. Her mind was transforming into a machine that navigated the road and moved edibles into her mouth. We had left the city. She was getting very into the moment. I think that she had had enough philosophy for the day. Along with her plastique food, she was digesting the idea that we live in a society, the freeway, a society, morals, food, society, freeway, conscience, food, . . . she trailed into a stupor.

I have always thought that a good dose of artistic nationalism instills pride in students. It gives them something higher than themselves to be loyal towards; it thus provides morals and an energizing sense of duty. Marguerite was being American by keeping her eye upon the wheel and drawing inward. As, she withdrew from me

I hoped she occasionally thought about what American character might be like. I began to fade.

Curiously, she did not call me back for some time. Of course, that saddened me. But, it also contained a bittersweet element. It was a sign of Marguerite maturing. She was becoming more of an independent thinker. And this, both as a father figure and an educator, gave me a great sense of satisfaction. At least that is what I hoped kept her mind off of me. Regardless, even as I faded, I appreciated all the time I had been able to spend with her, on this earth, fully conscious.

Suddenly, I found myself out in the middle of a wind-swept desert. I pulled with my nose as though inhaling a deep breath of this sky and wide landscape. I was somewhere on earth. Though I still went through objects as illusions, I thought I could actually sense some friction in my empty breaths. Even with such minimal results, these breaths brought me great peace.

Then I heard some rattling at my feet. Like a lizard, instinctually, I looked down. And, under a rock, wouldn't you know, were a notebook and a pen. I picked up the notebook and looked inside. All the notes I had previously written about my time with Marguerite were organized inside.

Being assigned to Marguerite was not random; this was no ordinary guiding assignment. I had no idea why I had been given so much time with her. But, I knew what I was meant to do. Relaxed and reassured, I picked up the pen and began to write.

CHAPTER
~ 14 ~

CRITICISM

"Howdy stranger!" Marguerite startled me. My delight in seeing her was only dampened by my the fact that I only needed to write about two more pages to get me up to the beginning of our traveling.

When you live as a writer with a day job - a traveling day job, with trains to catch, wherein you must find new restaurants and lodgings nearly every day - you come to horde minutes, and rush to get to endings. And, you get used to having your work interrupted. As quickly as I had been summoned to the desert, I now returned.

"How now, my Dearest Fresh Marguerite?" I stood up in the chair of the moving car and bowed as if illustrating Samuel 3:8-10, 'Speak; your servant is listening.'

"I'm sorry."

"My Darling Heart, whatever for?" I said, drifting down into my seat.

"I drifted off into thought and they took you away."

"Well, not to worry Love. I had a great deal of writing time in a desert. Really! I found myself in a desert with writing supplies as soon as I faded away. It was wonderful." I displayed a broad smile. She barely grinned as she shielded her eyes from the sun with her left hand.

She looked terrible. Her clothes were getting stiff and her long hair had seeds of clumps. I don't think she'd pulled over the entire time I was gone. My velvet coat, with its gold buttons, was, however, none the worse for wear. I looked, thank God, immaculate.

"Did you write about us?" She asked, again without looking towards me, her left hand still up shading her eyes.

"Yes, My Dearest Love. I have decided that that is why I am here, as your guide. I am not only to guide you, but to chronicle our adventures."

"Well, that would explain the writing supplies in the desert!"

"Yes, quite. So, actually, Darling Angel, I am not sure that your thoughts or lack there of, had anything to do with my disappearance. It may not be your fault. Remember, I'm dead. And, at any moment . . ." I let the ellipse finish its message of futility itself.

Honestly, though, I think I might have been a bit depressed. Because, at some level, I really did feel like she had forgotten about me and thus let me slip away from the world. Even if she were fixated on driving, she shouldn't have.

"That's true. But, . . ." The sun out of her eyes, she put two hands on the wheel.

"You know, Marguerite, you're dead too." She gasped slightly – her breath stopping for a moment. "I am sorry, I am in a bit of a pout. And, eventually I will be forgotten. I know that. But, you too should understand how fast all of this will disappear, 'A wind of promise and repose; From the far grave, to which it goes.' You too will die, my young friend. Appreciate your life."

We were in the middle of nowhere and far from civilization. The expanse of random rocks leading out to vast expanses of nothingness, the dust in the horizon, spoke to me. "I love nature, though it be deaf. I don't mean to put a point on it, but I always wonder if nature has any meaning other than that which we put on it. 'We ask and ask—Thou, nature, smilest and art still.' Its silence mocks."

"You, Sir, are profound." I knew I was being a bit of a sour puss. Intuitively, Marguerite turned to me with reassurance, "Really! I mean it. I love that about you. I think you could speak in poetry all day."

"Thank you for appreciating the place of mind in this vast, amazing, blank canvas."

"It is," my young apprentice offered, "amazing that these small towns pop – up in the middle of nowhere. It seems so weird that they're out here in the middle of nowhere. I keep wondering how they got here."

"In one sense, My Grasping Love, real people built them. Pioneers: People on wagons. In another sense, they appeared as an act of pure imagination - thought manifest. And their shapes, . . . they aren't just wigwams, they are an entirely different idea. But, they are just that, ideas."

"It's kind of depressing." She contributed, "It makes them seem so, like nothing, just thoughts."

"Well, that's one possible reaction. Another is to appreciate the importance of thoughts to making cities and nations. If people cease to hold up our civilization as an ideal, it will begin to rot. The towns will fade, as I did when I was forgotten."

At that she turned to show me a sad, pouty look.

"Okay, yes," I confirmed, "I am still somewhat miffed, Love."

"I am sorry I left you on the side of the road." Marguerite repeated, holding her breath as a sort of self-punishment.

"Well, Marguerite, let's have none of that." I replied, "The way we best keep up our civilization is by exemplifying the very characteristics of a civilized people – the bricks of civilization. Let me, my dearest Little One, see a bit of dandyism."

"Can you guess what I had for breakfast, My Dearest Sweet Love Heart?" She began.

"Caviar, My Dear?" I guessed.

CRITICISM

"No, Daaaahling sweetness and light. Sweetness and light and sweetness and light with a side of sweetness and light."

"Oh yes, Sweetness!" I nearly yelled. "That was my morning dish all week, with 'the best that has been thought and said' as a wicked little dessert."

"Let's write a poem about that breakfast. Shall we My Enchanted Loveliest?" She queried.

"Oh no Dear, we shan't write about anything so petty as our own experiences. That's what ails your poems."

At that, our playful feeling went into a vacuum. "What! My poems? Have you read my poems?"

"Yes My Darling Sweetness. But, only until I determined the weaknesses they all exhibited."

"And how many poems did that take?" The delicate new artist demanded.

"Three."

"Woao!" She indignantly exhaled.

"My Dearest Heart. Relax. You're a seventeen-year-old American. Develop some grace in receiving criticism or you'll be eaten to shreds. This too shall pass, all life is a game. Don't get caught up. Play, like Hamlet. Play like you're playing in a play within a play."

"Okay. I'm just self-conscious."

"Let's look at this one," I said, in tutor mode, manifesting her poem. If she weren't driving, Marguerite would have hid her head in embarrassment.

**"This library is a grave,
The students are all slaves,
Social fashion,
Empty passion,
I hate it all."**

**"I just want to scream,
Wake me from this nightmare dream,
Time to awake,
It's a mistake,
Clear the halls.**

**"Sometimes the school walls,
Just kick me in my female balls,
Super model,
Plastic bottle,
All too tall.**

"At some level Marguerite, I love it. It is the best poem I have ever read."

"Shut up. Oh My Gawd, I am so embarrassed."

"No I love it because it comes from you, Darling! And it has so much heart. You tried. I love it." She didn't seem to think these compliments were anything but patronizing. "Really! You have a sense of rhyme and meter." I added for reassurance.

"I made the pattern up myself," She stated with heavily guarded pride.

"Well in university, when you study European literature, you'll learn about other meters."

"What makes you think I'll go to university or study European literature?"

"Well, let's just say that with poetic tendencies such as yours, you must write, Love. Writing is the source of your life of the mind, which, I noted, you have. A life of the mind is at the core of what it means to be alive. You know this. You will study European literature to enhance your mind. You must. You will."

Seeming buoyed by my encouragement, she played along perfectly. "Okay, then let's start now. What is wrong with my poem? And, don't worry about hurting my feelings. I'll swallow my pride."

"No. I'll not discuss your particular poem. I am going to give you ideals – general ideals to work towards. That is more helpful."

"Okay. What's one ideal then?"

"Poems should explore some specific deep question. The Marguerite poem we discussed looks at our universal estrangement from each other and the death of God; *Resignation*, the role of the poet and our relationship to time."

"Bad ass." She said nodding with an unguarded reverence. There was something onerous about being a role model. But, it made me feel important. I love that feeling. Then, recoiling, she pouted, "I guess my boredom in the library isn't so deep a topic."

"Marguerite, Darling, Love, you've got to be tougher. You're a young person. You've not had a single real literary criticism course. And, no, your course with that buffoon, Mr. Early, does not count."
As she still looked a bit pouty, I added, "Play with me Marguerite. We'll have some fun in thought land. If you're into the life of the mind, playing in thought land is very, very," and I hesitated before saying it, "bad ass!"

With that transgression, she smirked.

"May I provide you with another ideal, my Brave Young Companion?"

"Hit me with it." She nodded resolutely.

"Well Love, I argued that poetry should portray historical moments. A great human action of a thousand years ago is more interesting than a small human action of today. By invoking great historical moments, we lift people out of their own times. They then get used to surveying history. When they do so, they cannot but help to admire the clear minds of the Greeks, and admire the length of their own civilization."

"Hmmn," Marguerite absorbed this information, "I guess my writing about my boredom in a high school library is pretty much just in my time."

"And another thing, and here I'm not asking, is that your poems should have stories. My contemporaries, Wordsworth and the Romantics, wrote like you, mostly just wrote down their thoughts as they came; they did not tell stories."

"Wait a minute!" Marguerite shrieked. "The Marguerite poem isn't Greek. And, now that I think about it, the Resignation poem, where you and your sister are looking back on being in the same park as children, isn't some great historical moment either; It's you walking in a park."

"Darling, I abhor pure system. I am giving you beautiful ideals. They aren't meant to cramp you, but expand you. I have many lovely ideals. But not every poem or moment of life must live up to them. That would be very stiff."

"Okay, hit me with another ideal!"

"Your poems should always be uplifting and help society."

"Oh, you mean like the Empedocles poem about a Romantic committing suicide?" Marguerite was playful, but seriously annoyed at the discrepancy.

"Darling, Sweet, Marguerite," I said with a humorous pleading, "You are entirely too sharp. Did you know that?"

"Aw shucks," She blushed.

"That isn't fair. You can't use my poems against me. Besides, I withdrew Empedocles from circulation."

"What!"

"Yes. It *was* too depressing. It just brooded on problems and gave us nothing to do."

"But Empedocles was beautiful." She endearingly defended my poem. "I love the idea that our thoughts are separate from the world and that they're little and we're trapped in them . . . You just said ideals shouldn't choke out your art and you choked out Empedocles. Oh my God!"

"I changed my mind. You should study law in university." I smiled. "And, in my defense, I learned about taking ideals too seriously later in life. And after that I republished Empedocles."

"Good!" She smirked with obvious satisfaction.

"In fact, though, . . . to be perfectly honest . . . "

"Yeah." Marguerite encouraged me, sensing blood.

"You're right. I pretty much even failed to live up to my ideal of not letting strict ideals tie you down."

"Really." She appreciated my honesty.

"Really. I think critics who say that my poetry got stiff as it tried to live up to my lofty ideals, were right. I let my ideals make my poems stiff. My poems just became illustrations of my ideals."

"Oh, that's a shame."

"No. It's okay. 'Youth had finished its tedious vain expanse, of passions that for ever ebb and flow.' You need an emotional, passionate – dare I say it? – even a romantic spirit, to write great poetry. That spirit had left me. I was a worker."

CRITICISM

"Well that's a nice admission, Mr. Arnold."

"Writing poetry got to be less and less fun. That's why I sort of gave up. All my final poems were just tributes to my dead pets: my dog, my bird."

"Aww, how cute."

"Yes, cute. But, not quite the lofty, uplifting exploration of great Greek themes I argued for." I said, looking away dejectedly.

"Now who needs a thick skin?"

"Oh, please let an old and dead man enjoy his sulk, won't you?" I smiled with strained ironic effort.

"I did sometimes have a thin skin. But I never showed anything but a light, banter quality in my public replies. I had a trick. You know how I kept my replies light?

"Nope. How?"

"I didn't look at criticisms of my work until weeks after they had been published. By that time I had always moved on a bit. And, also, if you wait for all the criticisms to air before responding, the opposition will have put all of their cards on the table."

"Good strategy."

"And the most, very most important thing."

"Is . . ?"

"Be ready to apologize if you're wrong."

Marguerite hadn't been expecting that. But, it seemed honest. It was honest.

"If I hurt someone's feelings in battle, I apologized as best as I could. I didn't reprint my book *On Translating Homer*, because it hurt someone's feelings more than I had intended. Partially, that was, of course, their fault, because their argument was so idiotic."

"I'm sure." Marguerite retorted only partially sardonically.

"No really. Newman was a total dunce, and the mark of a dying civilization. In his Homer translation he tried to drag noble Homer down to our level, to be 'faithful' and 'accurate,' instead of ascending towards Homer's Greek spirit of nobility, their grand style. Newman's petty realism was destroying the West."

"Wow."

"Really. I take criticism as seriously as that. To appreciate art, is to appreciate life, and both require a civilization, a culture of standards, beauty to behold. Criticism is life itself."

"Darn." She was back to being too adoring.

"Which is why, again, My Budding Flower, ideals shouldn't choke the life out of you. You should always have fun, as you obviously did writing your poem – 'kick me in my female balls.' Oh My Gawd." I laughed heartily.

"I'll tell you one more important thing, my young charge."

"One more?" She said comically, briefly taking her eyes off the road to confirm her interest.

"Yes, just one more."

"Well?" She playfully shrugged.

"Know that critics are your friends – your best friends. They flatter you just by letting you know that someone is listening. And, because I took critics' concerns seriously, they vastly improved my arguments, really. We had a wonderful time exploring the life of the mind together.
 "And sometimes . . ." I began laughing, "Well, one person wrote a terrific spoof of me using a character from my book *Friendship's Garland*, the one who represented me. He imitated me perfectly. I don't think I'd ever laughed so hard. Such good fun."

"I love that you can laugh so heartily about criticism. You have a wonderful perspective."

"Thank you Love Heart. Life is very short. And, being a public intellectual is a wonderful game. The life of the mind! What could be more fun? . . . outside of tennis or playing with your kids or dogs or . . . ?"

"It's nice to be around such a happy person."

"I return the compliment!" I said, proud of my influence since our first meetings.

"And, think about this, my young charge. If critics hadn't played along, if no one remembered me, well, I wouldn't be around to guide you."

"That's true."

"How wonderful; Literary criticism brings the dead back to life. As Job cried in recrimination, 'Oh that my words were now written! Oh that they were printed in a book! That they were graven with an iron pen and lead in the rock forever.' Literature, it allows you to argue with dead people!"

Marguerite didn't know what to do with that. I didn't blame her. Sometimes my bitterness and appreciation joined so closely I couldn't tell them apart myself. I actually loved the ache my awareness of death gave me. 'C'est la vie,' was a motto I savored. I paused and savored it.

The sun was going down and it was all two-handed driving from now on. My Captain, oh Capitan, she didn't have anything to add. Her elbows protruding upward from the too-large-for-her steering wheel, the conversation seemed complete. So she went silent and put her full concentration back on the road.

Still I could tell that she was making an effort to keep me in her mind so that I wouldn't disappear again. Someday, when this mysterious mission was finished, the powers would end my extended visit. I would disappear. But, I appreciated her effort to make me stay while she could.

To relax my fatigued driver, I manifested a piece of paper and a pen. "Darling Dearest, if you don't mind, I am going to take a minute to write."

"Not at all."

"And, if you have anything you wish to discuss, please ask. As and old traveling school inspector, I am the master of interrupted writing. It's actually a nice way to write. So, don't worry about interrupting me. But, until then, don't worry about forgetting me either, I'll write in peace." Yes, the R.I.P pun was intended!

She smiled coyly, "Aw My Dear Sweetest Mr. Arnold, don't worry. I won't forget you. You'll be in my mind every time I write, offering me ideals and criticism – even if from the dead. And, if I forget you momentarily, well . . . C'est la vie!"

Not only had I been in her thoughts, she'd been in mine.

CHAPTER
~ 15 ~

HOMESICKNESS

"Look! The West View Mobile Home Park!'" Marguerite shrieked, hitting the seat where my leg should have been and bringing me back from my second trip to the desert, back to the passenger seat. We had arrived at the trailer park of Marguerite's biological mother, the woman who gave her up for adoption, Twinkie.

"237, 237, way out back," Marguerite nervously repeated to herself as she drove us down a road, out past the main concentration of trailers. The feeling that the sound of the tires on the gravel implied, made me want to giggle. Finally, a bit down the road, we saw a trailer with so many people around it we knew we had arrived.

As we pulled up, I saw her mother on the porch. I was sure it was her because she looked so much like my Marguerite. She was also the only person get up and walk towards us. In more detail, she rose up, took a cigarette out of her mouth and threw it on the ground, took a drink from her big plastic cup, clutched it in both hands, and walked towards us.

Marguerite's biological mother was a fright and perhaps the ghost-of-Marguerite-future. She had dyed her hair blonde to the point of alopecia; she was older and frailer than Marguerite expected – beleaguered. As Marguerite's mother approached, her jerky round hip movement let you know she had physical pain. She had lingering cerebral palsy. She was also a little drunk, here in this, the early afternoon.

"Oh my baby I am glad to meet you at long last," the lady said. They hugged and held each other for a long time. A clinging desperation exuded from the hollow core of Marguerite's biological mother. And Marguerite found herself trying to escape this person's clutches, but was trapped in her belly and chest.

As my little companion felt herself being held, waves of sadness and anger fought in her head and heart. Panic and desperation happened. Finally she gave up trying to get free of the suffocating, needy clutches. But, when finally let go of, Marguerite emerged resolute and cold.

My poor Marguerite had been hurt for a long time. While slowly leaving victimhood behind, she still wrestled with the depressed and pensive young girl, inside of her, that I had met, weeks ago. She stiffened to coldness. Her victimhood needed to be forcibly shut out.

Her mother had cried during their embrace. She wore quite a bit of makeup that, especially around the eyes, seemed alien to Marguerite. Her running mascara touched my heart. Marguerite just studied the mascara as if it were a geology demonstration.

Marguerite rejected the pain of the woman's life and denounced the thousand years of alcohol-soaked tears in her eyes. My empathy with Marguerite put a freeze on any burgeoning fondness for Twinkie. Marguerite had never expected to feel such a disconnection, a lack of empathy for her mother. Judgment was happening.

They both had the same wide head that made the trajectory to their pointy chin look like a triangle. Both had a tiny button of a nose and small, taut mouth. And mostly, underneath the make-up, and beyond the distortion wrought from decades of drinking and smoking, Marguerite recognized the eyes - they were hers.

Marguerite cringed, and quickly looked away, deeply disturbed by the thought that her eyes could be in someone else's head. This meant her eyes weren't hers.

So this was my charge's alternate universe - the path not taken. Even as an atheist, my charge sub-vocalized 'Thank you,' to the universe. At the same time, there was the moment to tend to. It was awkward.

"Twinkie?"

"Well, you don't have to call me 'Ma' as I ain't your Ma a sorts. But, I am, I am so nervous, I cain't tell you. It makes me shake . . . shake more than I usually do." Twinkie said, making fun of her own palsy. "And I don't have to tell you that I have been a wreck, more of a wreck than normal, lately; waitin' for your ass to get here. A sorry wreck."

Marguerite's mother hit her consonants with force and had a drawl that smoothed out the shaking in her voice. After a small cackle she explained, "I want you to come up to the porch and meet your brothers and sister."
'Half-brothers and sister,' I most certainly heard Marguerite mutter. 'Conduct,' she started repeating with a desperate mantra-like repetition, 'is four-fifths of life.' 'Remember conduct, remember charm.' 'Sweetness and light.' After a hard push of will, Marguerite expelled two more words, "Of course."

That done, Twinkie reached down to get her large plastic cup of – we could only assume – alcohol. Marguerite had never had a compulsion to drink or smoke. Reflecting on her abstinence, she felt a sense of relief. She didn't want to be related to this family or in this situation in any way. Twinkie grabbed Marguerite's hand and turned to walk.

Holding Twinkie's hand and walking required that Marguerite slow down and adjust to the rhythm of the older woman's limp. She felt her arm pull and push in reaction to the feel of the woman's grasp. When Twinkie turned back to check on her, Marguerite didn't look at her eyes. And she didn't want to see the people down the driveway. She disconnected her mind from her eyes so that while she looked at everything, emotionally she saw nothing. Anyhow, they weren't her eyes, she angrily reminded herself.

Marguerite wondered if Twinkie felt guilty for abandoning her as an infant or if she was just so darned focused on the prize she was bringing her real family that she already didn't have time for her again.

At about fifteen feet from the trailer, Twinkie let go of Marguerite's hand and walked on to grab family members.

Marguerite's mother had a very large buttock. It was so large that it was heart shaped. The corners went up above her waist on their own. 'Oh My God,' Marguerite thought, 'Will I have an ass that big someday? I will never let that happen!' Again, her outward vision faded to near black as she retreated inward.

As we approached, with me walking behind the scene, our height caught my attention. At 5'6" and 6'2" Marguerite and I were noticeably taller than anyone else assembled. No one could see me but the dogs, who stood curiously at abeyance at the sight of me. For her part, understandably, Marguerite did not turn around to register my reaction to any of this. Not needed, I gave some attention to the slight, real or imagined, feel of walking on a gravel road. What if?

"She has so many children, this mother." Marguerite told herself with clarity that she seldom exuded even when she purposely spoke to me psychically. "Five children with four men. Disgusting. Am I just another throw away out of this woman's womb? One of her shits?" Her eyes darting between Twinkie, the waiting relatives and assembled guests mirrored the pace of her thoughts. "Did this woman spend much more time with any of her men than she did with me? Does she think people are just garbage you throw away?"

The large crowd around the trailer appeared as zombies waiting to devour Marguerite's flesh. It reminded me of the Irish-potato-famine-inspired horror novels of my era.

The mobile home they sat around was about forty feet long. Silver panels lined its top half. The bottom half's panels were the brownish yellow of slightly spoiled bananas. Scrapes, dirt and dents tied the silver and yellowish halves together. On the left side, three small slat windows and on the right, a regular window provided ventilation. And in the center, four steps raised to a torn screen that partially shielded a door.

A girl just a bit younger than Marguerite, who had been sitting on the stairs, stood up as we approached. Marguerite recognized her. She winced, "Christina?"

"Yep." She confirmed.

"I recognize you from facebook." Other than being shorter, chubbier and more voluptuous, she looked remarkably similar to Marguerite.

"You're prettier than yer picture." Christina spontaneously offered. "So tall."

"Gee. Thanks." Marguerite could not return the compliment. Her stomach was grinding and her head spun. After a pause, she apologetically replied, "We look alike." 'Charm, charm,' she thought nervously.

"Yep we do." Christina loquaciously confirmed.

Three boys came forward: One about eleven, and two younger dark-skinned boys, of about the same age. They – Marguerite guessed correctly – were her half-brothers.

An older woman stood up, threw her lit cigarette to the ground, exhaled a cloud of smoke and walked towards Marguerite. She introduced herself as Aunt Beanie. As awkward attempts at handshakes led to hugs, at a distance, nine or so people, kids included, just watched as if they were in an audience.

'Trailer parks gossip,' Marguerite reckoned. About half of the adult onlookers had cigarettes and all had plastic cups or bottles next to them. Their slouches indicated intoxication. The people's pasty white complexions and faded clothes gave an impression of insularity. The group greatly reminded me of the impoverished people I encountered, as a school inspector, in East London.

Animals love me. And, having adjusted to the translucent man, two dogs now came to play with me. I wished to focus on the scene at hand. So I squatted to pet them as I looked on. Maybe it is the same for all guides (though I suspect it is only me), but whereas my hand goes through people and I can only feel light intimations of objects, I can touch animals.

The crowd wondered why the two dogs lay on their backs as if they were having their bellies petted. Mentioning this distraction reduced the awkwardness as the flurry of introductions melted into silence.

The crowd ate burgers, chips, and hot dogs. And they all really wanted Marguerite to drink beer. She refused, now more than ever. Likely via Christina, word had gotten out that Marguerite's father worked on a show that they watched, *Ted's Home*. This made Marguerite royalty.

The men obscenely joked about sexual horrors they wished to inflict on the female stars of the show. The women probed Marguerite for inside information on these celebrities, only one or two of whom Marguerite had met in passing. Her explanation of these short encounters met with earnest, serious attention. Then the crowd burst out repeating the stories to each other, boisterously speculating on details as if Marguerite weren't there.

Christina looked embarrassed that she'd leaked this information. That's how I know she did it. She didn't say anything else to Marguerite – other than asking her to pass foods – the rest of our afternoon there. Marguerite understood the awkwardness. She didn't have the heart to tell Christina or the crowd that she had actually not watched any of the shows her father worked on.

Pure snobbery did not keep her from her father's shows. I realized then that Marguerite was actually jealous of the time and dedication her father gave to the shows rather than to her. And, it became clear that this came from prior abandonments, (including the one she was confronting here and now). The nervous attention on the shows and celebrities gave Marguerite a buffer, some space within which to stabilize herself. She faked interest and pretended she had seen the show as they recounted episodes.

Possibly the only time in following two hours that Marguerite actually looked at me came when the first person called her father's show, 'Ted's Home,' 'Ted is Home;' misconstruing the possessive apostrophe. Marguerite psychically, on purpose or not, let me know that her father's production company had encouraged this grammatical misinterpretation by making, 'Ted is Home,' the catchphrase for the show. This tactic had worked seamlessly with Marguerite's new clan.

As quickly as Marguerite acknowledged this factoid to me, she went back into her daze. Each time a family member said the magic phrase, I thought about Marguerite's mention of the grammatical error and noted her face growing tauter and paler.

Only just having met Marguerite for the first time, the crowd didn't know that her skin color usually had red overtones. Ghost white, as her skin blanched, Marguerite's few blemishes seemed to get redder by contrast.

As the sun went down, the crowd dispersed and Christina had to take her only opportunity for a ride to her father's house. She left awkwardly with a shy wave, accompanied by a still guilty-seeming, "nice to meet you," from about six feet away. She turned around after Marguerite's languidly waved back, walked across about twenty feet of gravel, got in the interior-lit passenger seat of a red car and drove off.

Only Twinkie, the two darker young half-brothers, Aunt Beanie, and about five other guests remained. Reduced to a much smaller circle, we retired to the living room to watch television.

A man brought out a folding chair for Marguerite. But, otherwise, everyone already had their designated seats. I hovered snuggly between Twinkie's recliner and the couch.

The pervasive television flicker made the room look strangely like it sat in an approaching lightening storm. The occasional eruptions of laugh tracks, sounding curiously like thunder, reinforced the stormy image. But, to my ear, nothing sounded louder than the heavy tick of the square wall clock. The moonlight entering the window, helped the television's flickering highlight millions of dust particles hanging, nearly immobile, as if suspended in a closed crypt.

"Might we?" I startled my mesmerized charge.

"Yes, before I suffocate." But, she pleaded, "We have to wait until the end of this show; this is 'Ted is Home.'"

And stated, with all frustration and no humor, "I am sure they'll get angry if I leave before it ends."

"Yes. Yes." I agreed, "I am sure they'll wish to tell their friends that they watched this programming with the producer's daughter. It will raise their social standing throughout the wider trailer park community." I winked with a devilish humor that, I detected, had negligible impact.

"Assistant producer."

"Thank you." I returned dryly, without affect.

Unable to extricate ourselves, we spent the night there. At one point there was even talk of our spending a second night there. On the second day, the television went on as soon as the sun rose and the drinking commenced just a tad after. No one had a job, and so, aside from a single journey to the store, everyone stayed close to the trailer. In the morning they ate cereal. In the afternoon, they ordered a pizza - drinking and smoking all the while.

Around noon, I went for a walk in the nearby woods. Ever since childhood, I have loved nature and sports. Tennis, hunting, and fishing are my passions. I needed to take this oh-so-rare opportunity to stand alone in nature again.

I had always loved going back to Fox How, my childhood home. Even up until the end of my life, I went there to see my widowed mother and spinster sister. Besides wanting to see them, I returned to Fox How because I considered the woods themselves my extended family – my home.

I thought of my 'Lines Written in Kensington Gardens,'

> 'Here at my feet what wonders pass,
>
> What endless, active life is here!
>
> What blowing daisies, fragrant grass!
>
> An air-stirr'd forest, fresh and clear.'

It was early prose, insipid. Yet somehow, it now struck me as innocent and, so, beautiful in its simple freshness.

Knowing that I couldn't be hurt, I climbed up a tree. From my perch, of near about 10 meters high, I spied a rabbit and a deer. And I could see all the way out to the main road from whence we had come.

I thought of her family's main road as they might see it. As Akron was about a thirty-five minute drive yet. And, as I did not think Marguerite's 'family' traveled that far, they might call it, 'the road that goes forever in both ways.' It reminded me of the Middle Ages conception of Europe being flat earth encircled by water. The road defined their limits.

I spied a sparrow's nest in an adjacent tree. On the right side of my tree was a wren's nest. The mother brought the fledglings grub. Magically, as I spoke a brace of ducks, perhaps twenty, struggled by, pumping, in the sky.

George Sand, in her later life, worshipped the peasant too much. Yet, the peasants' seasonal planting and harvesting put them in touch with nature in a profound way. In 'Kensington Gardens,' as Sand claimed, I made the case that peasants did not realize their own beauty as much as passers by did.

'Yet here is peace for ever new!
When I who watch them am away,
Still all things in this glade go through
The changes of their quiet day.'

But unfortunately, I could see no such nobility in the modern American peasant. They produce nothing and consume trash without conscience. The entire time I eavesdropped, Marguerite's family entertained no topics concerning anything but consumption – largely media consumption.

If I lived here I would definitely hunt and fish for food. That rabbit would be in trouble! As modern culture would never furnish such a thought, Marguerite's kin sat in recliners, generations together, watching staged wrestling. The all-too-obvious irony of people in such ill health watching athletics saddened me.

"But, enough of them," I thought. I so rarely have an opportunity to enjoy earth. I closed my eyes and felt the sun beating on my forehead. A small amount of sweat tickled my sideburns. Real sweat! And, air, I was nearly sure, filled my lungs. The sound of the leaves crescendoed and waned. Both the earth and I appeared to be breathing together.

Then the winds seemed to rise without ebbing. Rather they jolted back and forth as they rose. They got stronger and grew stronger as if gasping. Then, as if choking, the branches began to convulse violently. Panicked, straining to a lower branch, my footing failed, I fell.

And, I felt branches, somewhat, I thought, as I fell straight down and landed in the passenger seat of Marguerite's car. She sat in the driver's seat sobbing so loudly that she didn't seem to notice my appearance. Instantaneously, I knew that the jerking of the wind in the trees was the jerking of her sobbing.

"My poor Marguerite! My poor Marguerite! What happened?" I cried in anguished frustration, unable to reach her. How horrible it was to put my hand out to comfort this tender broken heart and have my person go through her as air.

I thought she still didn't register my presence when she burst, "Ahhh! What the fuck! I can't, I can't!" She went back to gasping.

"No, no, no Dearest. No need to speak. I cannot hold you, but feel comforted and speak when you will. I'm here and we have time." She cried for a good five minutes. During that time she produced some open mouth wails the like of which I had not heard since my wife wailed over the death of three of our children.

When our children died, my wife and I became so despondent that we had to escape. We went away to Italy. During that time, I didn't interact with the world. I couldn't write. My light touch abandoned me. Slowly, I ate that pain. I assimilated it, as if it were pre-existing; as I had assimilated knowing the strong possibility of my dying early, as my father and grandfather had.

And, in this situation, I froze. The tears remained inside. I cried at nearly everything since my death. But, this was too much. I froze. I paused. I waited. Eventually only

Marguerite's runny nose and sniffles lingered. She was regaining her breath and composure.

"Well, I found out who my real father is." She sunk, her bent posture fully forward and her stringy dirty hair hanging straight down.

"Yes?" I asked, conscientiously not exhaling.

"Oh God. I can't stand it. I can't even tell you. I can't. I can't." At that she burst into tears again.
"Well, when you're ready My Love."

"I'll never be ready to be ashamed, to be so fucking ashamed, to be so fucking ashamed for my whole fuckin' fuckin' life."

"Dear, do you know that I love you? I will never be ashamed of or anything but tender towards you." I looked at her mournfully, though she didn't look up. Now tears were welling up in my eyes as well.

"My father, . . . that Twinkie and I got talking, . . . Grblblru." I nodded, she continued, "That Twinkie doesn't even know who my father was. She kept referring to him as 'the cute guy from the KFC.'"

"What is the KFC?"

"A fast food chicken place; KFC is short for Kentucky Fried Chicken. We've passed many of them on the road. Their signs are big red and white buckets that turn in the sky."

Unfortunately, for some reason, this seemed very funny to me. I nearly laughed! But then I thought about just how wrong that would be and got control of myself. "You're only seeing humor in this because you can't deal with the pain," I repeated to myself. "Conduct."

She cut in, "All this time I had hoped that I came from somewhere worthwhile, somewhere interesting. Perhaps my father had an interesting hobby or an artistic talent. Maybe he was a writer. Maybe just strange. But, no, he is the fucking guy from the fucking KFC. My mother was a fourteen-year-old with palsy who fucked the guy from the KFC. How can I tell anybody that? How can I ever feel any pride in saying that? That's what I come from."
I nodded my head and kept listening, the urge to laugh had largely past. I understood this was a tragedy for Marguerite.

"She thought the guy from the KFC was cute. They got drunk. They fucked. After that she started fucking some other guy and she lost contact with the guy from the KFC. Only then did she realize she was pregnant. That's her story."

I nodded.

"And the fucking maniac thinks the story is cute. She told me four times how cute he was. 'The cute guy from the KFC,' I could have fucking killed her!"

"My Dear, my Dearest Marguerite. I understand. I think I understand."

"I didn't think it'd be like this." Marguerite pleaded.

"I have never had a reunion with strangers. What did you expect?"

"I don't know. But, at some level, I thought that I'd feel I belonged. I'd find that missing piece of me, that piece that says, 'You're home' would show up." She sniffled and finally looked up at me, "That's it. I have no home. I don't belong in this world, this fucking trashy world."

"Rubbish. Your father loves you very much. That man would kill for you, broken though he is."

"If he'd kill for me, why is he inviting that horrible woman into our home?"

"Dearest, people are frail. Your father has been through a lot. You saw him collapse when you suggested this trip, right?"

"Yeah. I've been thinking about that and how his life with Mom, er, Mother, must have been."

"And, did you notice the nasty glance you gave me when I said he was broken?"

"Yes."

"He's your father. That man has taken care of you and loved you your entire life. He saved you from this. He is your real father. Not the man from the chicken restaurant."

As Marguerite slumped and sniffled, I explained, "As for Samantha, she controls him because she is insecure. She has never felt loved. Her father left when she was just six. At some level she doesn't trust that your father will stay with her, so she is getting what she can while she can. But, give her time. Love her. She may relax; she may not. But, after some time, to the best of her ability, she too will come to love you."

Marguerite looked at me with a bit of horror. She wondered how I knew such things. I seemed like a demon to her. I had no idea where that string of facts came from. But, I knew them as I said them; I knew them as if I had always known them.

"But, even if she gets scared and leaves, you should never doubt that your father loves you more than anything in the universe. He will never leave you. He is your father, your real father. Not the man from the, uh, the uh . . . "

"KFC."

"Yes the KFC. It is an interesting nation and people, I'm sure. I've always wanted to visit the KFC, if only to try their cuisine. Perhaps after the USA." I joked. "Now the MFC, . . . I don't think I want to go there or eat their food. Greasy!" I screeched with real tears' moist residue on the sides of my nose.

"Thank you Mr. A."

"You're welcome Dearest." I said with a supercilious smile. "Darling, you know that I am a dandy and so routinely shoot for effect."

"Yes."

"I love the pose and think that conduct is four –fifths of life."

"Yes."

"Yes. But, do believe me when I tell you that, alongside

your father, I love you too. You're a jewel my darling young Marguerite."

"Thank you Matt. I love you too."

"Well isn't that just a little too much. How about a song?"

"A song?" She shot at me, bemused and confused.

"No?"

"Do you know anything from our century?"

"No. I only know hymns, disgusting English hymns, full of German flatness."

CHAPTER
~ 16 ~

CULTURE AND ANARCHY

Despite our occasional successes in achieving levity, the next day of driving had a somber edge to it. There were long times without discussion. I tried to write, but kept getting distracted by the gravity of the moment.

As such, my attention increasingly drifted out of the windows towards the surroundings. The Midwestern landscape has the feeling of a canvas. Its large openness invites reflection - awe.

But, town after town, as we rode up the interstate, filled me with a sense of mourning. I had failed to save America as I had failed to save England. My message briefly got adopted by Babbit and the "New Humanists" in the 1920s. But, . . .

I came to this country two times while I was alive. But the second time was really only to visit my daughter and new grandson. Wouldn't you know, Dear Reader, my daughter,

Lucy, fell in love with a New York banker while accompanying my lovely wife and I on my first tour. And, so, in a sense, not only did I fail to save America, I lost a daughter here too, to this.

My mournful attitude came from witnessing the brutal ugliness along the side of the highway. The McDonalds, malls, and KFCs (which I now saw everywhere), spoke to a singular brutal ugliness - a lowering of all humanity towards its basest instincts. I ruminated on how this brutality had played out in Marguerite's own family line.

Suddenly, I imagined a congruence between my three-part analysis of England and the bitter fruits of America that crystallized in Marguerite's family.

"Marguerite?"

"Yes, My Love?" The affirmation came wrapped in a pretended English accent. A detached tenderness could now be heard in her voice. She had a touching calm. She had changed, subtly, for the better. For that reason, I delayed a long time in bringing up the following subject.

"I wish to touch upon a, a, a touchy subject with you."

"My family?"

"Yes. It occurs to me that they illustrate a main theme my most widely-read book, *Culture and Anarchy*."

Junk food gone, relaxed, she bravely agreed, "Okay."

"And it is alright if you're offended. I am used to offending everybody. But what I have to say must be said. In my time I thought it vital for the public to hear.

Culture and Anarchy was really a collection of popular newspaper articles. And I think their theme will mean something to you. Besides it is burning a hole in my little skull and I need to express it."

"Well as long as you smile throughout, Dearest. You know, conduct is four-fifths of life." I found her imitations of my accent very endearing. She was perfectly absorbing my sense of poised calm, my philosophy of sweetness and light. I relished this teaching moment.

"Yes." I played, "Conduct is four-fifths of life. And, the other fifth . . . dairy – nothing but dairy."

"Quite so." She laughed, "dairy."

"Well, in *Culture and Anarchy* I detailed the dynamics of barbarians, philistines, and the populace."

"Okay, well, yeah," she searched her years, "I've heard of people calling people 'philistines.'

"Yes, I," I smirked with a haughty gesture towards myself, "I taught the West the phrase 'philistine.'

"So are my family members philistines?"

"Dear, please don't take this as anything less than sociological. I have already defended your father and think you'd do well to give him more love and empathy than you already do. Correct?"

"Yeah, you did." She sounded sincere, which gave her a childlike tone.

"And remember to smile little girl or I'll tickle you."

"You're dead. You can't touch things."   She smiled broadly.

"Thanks Love. So, to it, . . . Succinctly, the aristocracy were barbarians; the middle class were philistines; and the working class, the populace."

"Aristocracy, barbarians; the middle class, philistines; and working class, populace," she rehearsed.

"Precisely." I proudly confirmed.

"So lemme guess. My father is the middle class philistine and the Twinkie the working class populace."

"Give me some moments, now, and then you can guess. Alright?" With silent consent, her eyes on the road but her ears astute, I continued, "Aristocracy was a good thing. Shocking, I know," I exclaimed, obviously relishing the shock. "Traditionally, the aristocracy had the leisure to refine themselves in manner and learning. Their breeding set a tone for society, gave it standards, they modeled the fruits of being civilized."

"Yeah. Like your man, . . . what was his name, the guy who gave you freedom before you married Fluuuu?"

"Henry Petty-Fitzmaurice, the Third Marquis of Lansdowne, My Man Lansdowne. And, must you say my wife's name so sarcastically?"

"Sorry." She said, contritely.

"Though not flamboyant, or intellectual, my dearest Lovely Essential Flu made my life wonderful. We were married for thirty-seven years. She bore me six children.

She, more than anyone else, kept me from falling apart when three of them died in a year's time."

"Sorry." She said, more mournful this time.
She was just teasing me. I think I may have reacted too harshly to her taunts because I occasionally did regret leaving my dandy life behind. Talking of Lansdowne and my marriage was irritating me. Marguerite had not lost the sense of intuition children and dogs have – she felt my insecurity and instinctually poked at it.

"I'm sorry, I didn't mean to respond so severely." I was sincerely contrite. "Entirely my fault. And, anyhow, yes, My Man Lansdowne was a perfect aristocrat. He upheld civilization's highest ideals, via attitude, conduct, and learning."

"Oh, okay, I get it. So that's why you called aristocrats, 'barbarians.' They were supposed to make standards like your aristocrat man."

"Lansdowne."

"Yes. And, instead they were acting like barbarians, like the Mongols or something. Barbarians way inside the gates."

"Bravo. Sometimes you really impress me My Young Charge. Bravo. Yes, in my time the 'aristocrats' were in permanent decline and, as a class, they had become drunken and venal. And, if they were no longer going to model the refinement of conduct and mind that leisure allows, who would?"

"The middle class philistines?"

"Yes."

"They weren't up to your standards either?"

"Oh, Dear, the perils of standards! People joked that I wouldn't even approve of God after death!" We both laughed. "But, Dear One, it wasn't just that the middle class were not up to *my* standards, they were not up to any standards – standards that any that a civilized person would respect. They only chased money, and money, and money.

"And to this end, the middle class was enormously productive. But if you asked them about history or art or religion, they were essentially hollow. Had they had bad taste, it would have been fine. But, they had no taste for anything but eating, producing and buying more and more inanimate objects."

"Philistines!" Marguerites sarcastically uttered with mock disgust.

"Pure philistines." I replied with my nostrils closed and my chin pointed as high as I could get it.

"You don't really have a snide term for the lower class. 'The populace' isn't so cutting."

"Darling, your biological family did not shock me. I worked amongst the poor all my life. And though I wished to have had the leisure of the aristocracy, I, myself, properly belonged to the middle class, the philistine class. My salary barely supported my family.

"But, to the point, the poor amongst whom I worked, well they made dear Twinkie look like a queen. Those with power, the barbarians and philistines, needed to bear the blame for the poor peoples' lack of cultivation, lack of sweetness and light. They had failed to set an example and allowed poverty to fester."

"So we've solved the one piece: Twinkie is the populace, the working class."

"Yes, even though she doesn't have employment." I said, aware that my epiphany didn't provide perfect parallels.

"What are the other two?" She bravely asked.

"Well your father, in my schema, is like the aristocratic barbarian. And, thank you for not blinking from your inquisitive gaze as I said that." She nodded attentively, somewhat disturbed that I could see her face even as she looked forward at the road.

"Your father makes popular television programs. Like the aristocracy, this position gives him the direct responsibility for setting a cultural tone for America. Instead he glorifies debauchery and attaches no shame to ignorance."

"I can see that. In a way, he is to blame for the disgusting state of Twinkie, who is, after all, named after an advertised food product." She then thought silently of the impact of KFC and mass culture on her life.

"Bravo, my young charge, you're making a dispassionate analysis. Perhaps the powers-that-be knew what they were doing when they sent me to guide you after all." At that we both beamed bright smiles.

"So if my father is the aristocratic barbarian and Twinkie is the working class populace, who in my family is the middle class philistine?"

"Well no one in your family, really. Those who mange the KFCs of this world, the great corporations, are the middle class. Not specifically your biological father, but those who, . . . the values that set up the chain store / mall culture and all those trapped in it. This class, perhaps poorer now than middle class, defined my nation's mediocre values and controls yours.

"So that's it. All of society has turned to shit."

"Darling, Sweetness, My Flower, mind your vocabulary?" I asked nicely.

"Ok. Sorry. So everything has become . . . just simply horrid?

"My exact phrase is that industrialism, 'materializes our upper class, vulgarizes our middle class and brutalizes the lower class.'

"There is something beautiful in that. You do choose your words carefully." She allowed.

"Especially in public writing, Dear. No less a personage than the British Prime Minister, Disraeli, noted that I had a knack for slogans. 'Full of frippery,' he said. Though too frequent repetition often led to my writing by rote, like when one of your phonograph albums is scratched. But still, I love that my phrases, like, 'sweetness and light,' 'philistines,' and 'the best that has been thought and said,' continue to be used as touchstones for cultural self-improvement. They rang true then and they ring true now."

"And, 'philistine,' even if we don't use the phrase much, we all know what it means. I think most Americans have heard the phrase."

"So in *Culture and Anarchy*, I say that to defeat this class-based denigration, we must cultivate 'our best selves,' by seeking 'perfection.' These were other phrases that I brought into public discourse."

Speaking in my prophetic voice I nearly yodeled, "In this sense the men of culture are the true apostles of equality. The men of culture have a passion for diffusing, carrying from one end of society to the other, the best that has been thought and said in the world – collapsing the distinction between barbarian, philistine and populace."

"What a big hope," Marguerite said, innocently, without snide intent. "It is amazing that people would actually discuss these ideas in newspapers back then."

"Yes, magazines too. And I helped shape these Victorian discussions with my knack for picking popular subjects, fomenting controversy, and handy catchphrases."

"So that's what you'd have my father do with the media? All that?"

"Yes. But, truly, that can't happen until the entire culture is ready for such edification. The average Greek could follow Sophocles. That is the only reason he could be popular. Average drunken peasants followed Shakespeare in his day, imagine. Ages make the flowering of genius possible. And, critics cultivate this cultural soil."

"Wow! All that is in *Culture and Anarchy*?"

"No, that vision of cultural-cultivation-via-literary critic came earlier than *Culture and Anarchy*. By the time *Culture and Anarchy* came around, I largely replaced the idea of society being uplifted by literary criticism with the idea of us finding our best selves via public education."

"Oh, yeah, that great idea again." She said sarcastically.
"Well, I would, obviously, banish the Mr. Earlys from the system. But, yes, school remains a beautiful mechanism to cultivate minds, if used correctly; It can create pride and unity via promoting national high culture."

"Well, it's a plan, I guess." She said sardonically. I had great appreciation for this girl. It did an old man good to convey some of his most heavily debated ideas to a new generation – even if only to hear them summarily dismissed.

"Well, it wasn't my only plan, public schools. I mean I also wished to cultivate standards via an institution like the French Academy. That's a national organization that watches language and cultivates taste in France.

"Really?" She said, this time with near perfect sarcasm wherein she tried to sound sincerely impressed. A stranger might have believed she really thought my English Academy idea a good one – she was an adept.

"Yes, really. And, though the English rejected the idea of having an English Academy. I won on the topic of having publically funded schools. In England, having schools like yours for the poor was somewhat my doing!" At this I got a less dismissive acknowledgement. "And, my literary criticism, the whole field being partially my invention, set much of the tone for the Victorian era."

"You're amazing."

"Thank you Love. I appreciate your listening more than you know. By the way, I lied to you."

"Mmm?" She quizzically awaited the joke.

"It isn't dairy. Life is four-fifths conduct and one-fifth pillows."

"Okay, pillows it is," she played along.

"Yes, My Heart, pillows puffed to perfection." I generously and humorously affirmed.

CHAPTER
~ 17 ~

LIFE AND DEATH

Seemingly minutes after the next gas station break, we were driving through downtown Cleveland, Ohio. I remembered this city from my first visit to America. It vindicated *Culture and Anarchy*. The philistine captains of industry claimed that the western world's glory lay only in its industrial production. In reply, I sardonically asked the aristocracy if there would be any reason for Britain to continue existing if we ran out of coal. In America, there wasn't even an aristocracy to ask. Anyhow, Cleveland is the answer.

Once a bustling center of production, Cleveland had become an empty vessel. Small tourist trams take people around a vacant downtown. One 1880s era building has mottoes such as 'industry,' and 'prosperity' engraved around its side. The faux Roman façade at least gave the philistine temple a hint of history, of connection to the past to consciousness.

The glass buildings surrounding this monument to philistine values, confirmed the monstrous potential of money without any sense of history. Decorating with poor taste is a good definition of 'vulgar'. These modern buildings have no decoration. They don't even have enough substance to qualify as vulgar. These glass boxes represent man's death by science.

The city features two stadiums in which thousands of residents cheer men for hitting and throwing balls. It is a gross hollow expenditure, lacking any connection to mind, taste or history. No other public function connects the 'residents' ('citizens' implies too much active participation) of Cleveland to each other. I don't disparage people's desire to belong to or root for something. But, as all other loyalties have faded, in these stadiums we glimpsed the soul of a nation – and it is hollow.

Tourists come to see Cleveland's 'Rock and Roll Hall of Fame.' It memorializes an attempted musical revolution that happened long before Marguerite was born.

Being American, this movement lacked all historical perspective. People did not recognize its Romantic roots. As had happened before, when people got bored of the self-absorbed romantic search for meaningful, they degenerated into chaos. But, because Americans reject history, this rock movement did more damage than the earlier Romantic Movement. Unreformed, America's subsequent music promotes nothing shy of bestiality.

Thus, the 'rock' music shrine, this shrine to music for rocks, props up hollow icons of a failed search for meaning. The icons largely dead, the visitors largely old and fat, the culture ruined, I couldn't decide if this 'Hall of

Fame' more resembled a slaughterhouse or the hive of a plague-carrying swarm.

As I came into her view, I cheerfully greeted Marguerite. "Hello Loveliness."

"Hello, Mr. Arnold."

"Are you ready for another fun-filled day of trauma?"

Her smile stammered on her angst. She squeezed both her eyes as if to say, 'It will be alright.' I squeezed mine back. As we rode out of Cleveland's city center, the desolation of America hit me hard. I really do care for western civilization. And, this former center of industrial might was surrounded by mile after mile of abandoned buildings. It frightened me.

Fortunately, we eventually came to an area with some seemingly inhabited homes. Not long after, the streets of houses led to an area with both houses and apartments. The percentage of apartments quickly increased to near domination. Not long on, we found ourselves in an area that only had apartment buildings.

Marguerite broke her silence by announcing, "1702 Esther Avenue: Apt C. That's it. I remember it! Wish me luck." Her disappointment had turned back into excitement.

As the young, vulnerable, determined Marguerite walked across the cracked asphalt road to the apartment block, I followed her, breathlessly. I understand the need to face demons squarely. And Marguerite's facing things as they really were had already added calmness, (yes, along with a pinch of disillusionment), to her character. Though some good *could* come from this, I choked on my nerves.

Eventually, she stood in front of the door and looked back at me. I smiled a smile for support and waved my hand for encouragement. After several false starts, she knocked. After several minutes of silence, she knocked again. She would have left, but she could hear some movement inside. Finally a man's voice, Les Christianson's, asked, "Who is it?"

"It's Marguerite Buckby. Is Cindy there?"

"Who is it?"

"Marguerite Buckby. Maggie. Cindy's daughter. You remember me, Dr. Les, Cindy's daughter, Maggie. Is Cindy home?"

There was a bit more rustling and the door opened about six inches.

"Les! Dr. Les." Marguerite said with automatic excitement. She must have retained some memory of this man from childhood. Perhaps he had been less onerous then. But, he terrified me.

Les was tall, very white, very thin, and unshaven. He had tried to tuck his white sleeveless t-shirt into his pants. But, had, apparently, gotten distracted. He peered out from the mostly closed door, "Maggie?" he checked.

"Yes," she replied, politely looking at her mother's other half. When he opened the door he put his hand in front of his eyes, to shield them from the sun. He seemed to have not have been outside for some time.

"Wow. You don't look much like you used to." He made this observation as his eyes started darting back and forth, looking up and down the street, but not at her - this urchin he hadn't seen for years - through the ajar door.

Marguerite didn't mind his not looking her in the eye or acting quickly, as she wanted to get a glimpse inside the apartment. The visible living room looked like a cyclone had spun it. A stained couch was covered in litter: clothes, empty beer bottles, a spilled box of cereal. It stank.

She imagined her mother on the couch in that chaos. How had they survived in there? Then she noticed the marks on Les' arm – drugs! It had been worse than Marguerite had imagined or could imagine as a child.

"Maggie I," Les started, his eyes still darting back and forth nervously. And, right away she knew, - perhaps due to her mother not coming to the door, perhaps due to the needle marks on his arm or the smell of the apartment, - exactly what Les was going to say. "Maggie, your mother died maybe, I don't know, about a year ago, two years ago."

Upon hearing the end of this sentence, Marguerite gave Les a firm and resolute nod that he failed to see. She abruptly turned around and marched back to the car, her stone expression had not a hint of tears, not a hint of tears. Les did not follow her to deliver final sentiments from her mother or offer trinkets of comfort.

Actually, honestly, Marguerite felt a sense of relief. The death of her adopted mother left a void. But, the void had long been there sucking in attention. Now it was sealed. She was dead. It was done.

And, oddly enough, the void brought forth feelings of warmth. She felt real empathy – for the first time – proper empathy for her drug-addicted mother. She finally understood that Cindy's violence was not a response to her as a daughter. Cindy's slow suicide, it taking so long and being so violent, and continuing so long after Marguerite was gone, meant that her adopted mother's pain was all her own, having nothing to do with Marguerite.

Marguerite, got in the car, put on her sunglasses and began to drive. I let her drive in silence. I didn't even offer to wipe the dust off of her dark glasses. We left the horror of Cleveland and merging onto the freeway made our way to barren nature and wide horizons. Finally, she dropped a pebble into the silence, "You know, the amount of nothingness out here amazes me. We just fly by it - big sky country, for sure. It's all pointless. I like that."

"Look outward, to your side." I offered, looking out at the long flat expanse on my right, aware that she had a parallel view on her left. "Look to the horizon. Do you see how steady it is? I mean, yes, all of the terrain close to us flies by. But that point on the horizon, far, far way from us, stays in view for a while. It doesn't move."

"That's poetic. Does it have something to do with my mother's death?" She asked with resignation and soft bitterness.

"You know, Marguerite, I lost my father when I was twenty. And, while your mother was a thought – a distant memory, mine was my life. He was a stern oak under whom we all rested. When he died, that was when I finally felt the silence in nature." As my head tilt asked for acknowledgement, she nodded empathetically. "Fifteen years after his death I went back to the high school he led to greatness."

"Rugby?"

"Yes. Rugby. There he worked, to etch a name in the big picture, to stake a claim on the horizon, so to speak." She nodded again, while her eyes remained on the road. "Father sought to do something that would stay in view for a long while. Part of why I am so contemptuous of people is that they are so petty, so caught up in nothing.

"In my poem about father's death I wrote:"

What is the course of the life,

Of mortal men on the earth? –

Most men eddy about,

Here and there – eat and drink,

Chatter and love and hate,

Gather and squander, are raised,

Aloft, are hurl'd in the dust,

Striving blindly, achieving

Nothing; and then they die.

"That's beautiful. It's what I feel right now. My mother, my adopted mother, she basically killed herself, with the drugs and all. But, it wouldn't have made any difference to the world if she were still alive."

"It would have made a difference to you."

"Yes, but she and I are both like so much close-up scenery blazing by at a million miles an hour; like so much rubble on the side of the road. It wouldn't have made a difference in the big picture." Behind her dazed acceptance, cried-out sadness filled her vision of the long road ahead.

America was collapsing. People used to at least have the warmth of their families, and enough pride in their family-line to give their lives expanded meaning. Now, everyone was just an anonymous guy from the KFC, with temp jobs and temp families. We are ephemeral if we don't engage in something larger than our private lives. And, families had become very isolated from each other, more private. But, where they exist, families still provide something other than oneself to live for, attachments, and so morals. Marguerite's mother provided nothing.

"I won't disagree." I broke the long silence. "And, yet, in a way, I think your mother exceptionally great. She looked bleakness in the eye. She lived with an awareness of death, a feeling of it that many cheery people run from. And, as such, her death has given you the opportunity to look closely at death and meaninglessness. That is a real gain."

"Yeah, but she was ultimately very selfish. She dragged everyone else down to her level of despair. She was self-obsessed."

"And that's the way out, to not be self-obsessed." I replied earnestly. "Families give you a sense of belonging, of mattering. My father provided that. When he died, I felt the deep cavity of his absence. But, he was somehow, still always there, guiding me towards social goals. Nearly all of my work, especially after my marriage, reflected his priorities.

"And, in his short life, he changed the face of education in Europe. In fact, many of his students took positions of prominence in administering the British Empire. My brother William became the first head of education for the

Punjab, in India. It can really be said that my father influenced the world."

Marguerite, though she held her eyes firmly on the rode in front of her, was listening and was interested. And so I continued. "I found his earnestness, in the face of death, - him also knowing he was doomed to an early death, because his father died young - admirable."

"Oh," she connected life to art, "That poem where there was a good king who was going to die young and so partied, well your father is like the opposite of that, right?"

"Yes. My father was the opposite of Mycerinus."

"Yes. Mycerinus."

"And," stressing the connection, "it was largely because of my father's attitude, and the education that he provided me, that I strove to matter, to build structures that would outlast us all, to mark the horizon. So, after describing the hopeless masses, my 'Rugby' poem, my tribute to my father, continued:

Ah yes! Some of us strive

Not without action to die

Fruitless, but something to snatch

From dull oblivion, nor all

Glut the devouring grave!

We, we have chosen our path –

Path to a clear – purposed goal,

Path of advance!"

"That's beautiful too." Marguerite said, now slightly less tinted with sadness. "His struggle for meaning in front of the grave, dull oblivion."

"Well yes. But, the next stanza is very grim. It portrays life as a long walk through a treacherous valley. Many die on the way. But, though we stride forward, eventually we get to death's hotel. As we're exhausted from our journey, we cannot refuse his offer of lodging."

"That's creepy." She paused, "And, I like it. And, I like, that your work attacks public philosophical themes so often. And, I guess that your father's life did matter to the ages because the world still knows who he is. And, well, you're here with me. But, I don't now that I'll be remembered."

"I have a feeling you will be. If not to posterity, at least to a great and loving big family." Marguerite blushed at this.

"But, before that, always be kind to people, because they are all struggling in the face of death. My Dearest Lovely Essential Flu is scarcely ever conscious, due to her having only been remembered as my wife. My children, three of whom died in their youth, have entirely passed. No one remembers enough of them for them to have sustained consciousness in the afterlife."

"How do you know? Maybe they are alive. You still remember them."

"No, I feel it. I realize they've largely faded to oblivion. It doesn't make them any less important to me. I still cherish their memories, however vaguely formed. But, alas, the dead cannot sustain the dead." At that we luxuriated in silence for a moment.

Then still largely snuggled in silence, I muttered, "People say I overused natural images as symbols in my poems. But, I find them timeless."

"Yes, timeless," Marguerite mumbled looking out at the vast expansive plains, encircled by the horizon under the open sky.

As we silently drove farther, through these great desolate plains, Marguerite came to realize, with a strong but muted joy, that Cindy's death vindicated her father. There was no way that Marguerite could have stayed married to such a person either. Marguerite found room to forgive her father and even wept a bit as she silently drove. The divorce was not his fault.

But then horror struck her. What if her father's abandoning Cindy turned her into the druggie she became? What if he hadn't left Cindy? Would she still be alive; a nice mother to Marguerite? The drama of these questions hit her with potency stronger than the actual death had.

Then she saw her tortured, drug-addicted, dead mother in the shiny kitchen of her Hollywood home, waving her thin blue arm at Marguerite. The image seemed as real as a severed hand in daylight.

"Remember when I pointed out how hunched and pained your father looked when you suggested driving in this direction?" I interrupted.

"Yes." She replied, getting my point.

"Your father is a nice, if meek, man. He could not inflict that kind of pain with all his might. Cindy's self-torment preceded him by a long time, it was her own. It's amazing that your father kept her healthy and in domestic life as long as he did. She psychically wounded your father, not the reverse. You know this."

As a semi-truck got perilously close to our lane, she turned her head to acknowledge my insight.

"I'll give you more evidence," I offered, "He had the presence of mind to rescue you. He knew that being near such a collapsing black hole would only bring great harm upon you. He may not have saved the world, my Dear Marguerite. But your father saved you. He is a good man."

At that Marguerite turned off of an off ramp. At the light at the bottom of the ramp, she stopped the car and let loose a torrent of tears.

"It's okay Dearest," I said trying to comfort her, "It's okay. You're safe now. You survived this trip. You have a home to go back to and a long future ahead of you."

CHAPTER
~ 18 ~

THE CHURCH OF ARNOLD

"Marguerite?" I smiled wickedly.

"Yes, Mr. Arnold." She replied with a tongue-in-cheek attitude towards our formality. I realized that our formality was probably inappropriate by now. But, it had become an inside joke between the two of us. I was glad to have it so.

"Loving, Darling, Sweetest, Dearest, would you mind if we visited a place just a tad off the beaten track?"

"How far off the beaten track?" We had driven for less than an hour since leaving Cleveland, but the stress and days of driving were starting to wear on her, her hair was getting clumpier.

"It's only about an hour out of the way, Love. And we can stop there for the night, so that you won't have to drive much more after we arrive. Please!"
"Well, what sorta place?"

"It's a place I visited my first time in America."

"Well what kinda place?" She pressed.

"You'll see when we get there. It's a place has a lot of sentimental value for me. Isn't that enough?"

"Yes. For My Dearest Mr. Arnold, it is," she kindly relented.

My hesitance in telling her why I asked that we drive some eighty miles out of the way stemmed from the lack of enthusiasm modern young Americans have for churches. They would sooner go denture shopping with their ninety-year-old grandmother than step foot in a church.

As we maneuvered into the small white church's parking lot, Marguerite, true to form, whined, "A church?"

"Yes My Wonderful Companion, it has great sentimental value for me. And I predict that we're going to learn some valuable lessons here."

"That's good enough for me." Marguerite's best characteristic was her willingness – no, her blossoming commitment - to learning. Slamming her dusty brown car door, she waited for me to lead the way inside.

The church looked like a one-room schoolhouse. And for a reason that Marguerite could not yet fathom, they were having a Tuesday night service.

The audience was white and elderly, with only a hand full of racial and age-related exceptions, in a congregation of nearly one hundred. Many of the men the same sort of wool double – breasted suits I had on. Many of the women sported large brimmed hats with great big flowers on them. This group was far more eccentric than your normal Midwestern bingo set. They resonated with a different era.

The preacher himself had the same wide sideburns that I do. He even had a monocle – a single glasses lens on a chain – like the one I wore on my American tours. He put it on his right eye in preparation for speaking.

Even before he uttered his first words, Marguerite had a very unsettling and creepy feeling. A strong combination of revulsion and terror immediately ran through her body as the preacher began speaking.

"Do you know that Matthew Arnold visited this very church in 1883? And where I am standing right now, he provided us with an eloquent speech on the subject of religion. So eloquent, that we changed our focus from teaching old-fashioned Christianity to teaching Arnoldian Christianity."

In her sharp panic, Marguerite's voice became very distinct to me. Then her thoughts overtook mine, to the point where I could barely hear my own.

She emphatically charged, "Making me raise my hand in Mr. Early's class and playfully getting me to fight with him was somehow cute. But, taking over the preacher's body and using him like a puppet to preach to this crowd freaks me out." Speaking about me in a voice I could not muffle, she continued, "The preacher is a stranger. Have you gone mad? Human puppets?"

She continued, "Arnold is smiling one of his manic grins of enthusiasm. He looks insane and creepy. Oh my God. I'm gunna run away."

In deep revulsion, without any conscious input from her mind, Marguerite's left leg jerked upwards as if to run away. We both looked at each other as she talked her leg back into staying with her in the pulpit. This was not a dream; It was a waking nightmare for Marguerite. Her friend and mentor had gone insane with power, using a preacher like a puppet.

In fact, she realized, the entire congregation had to be there, at some level, from my controlling their minds. "Did the parishioners just coincidentally come to hear this speech, on a Tuesday night or could Arnold control the thoughts and actions of groups? No. This isn't normal. He's controlling them, all of them."

"Arnold once told me that people had stopped believing in the Bible. Therefore, going forward, poets and artists would have to provide society's emotional sources of moral inspiration. The artists, he said, would be the modern world's new religious figures. At the time, I loved the idea of artists taking religion's place. But, now I see he meant it literally – he's launching his poet-as-priest plan by taking over people's minds. I believe in free will, this is not right!"

Arnold gave me a very innocent grin and shrug that pleaded, 'Who me?' He had his normal attitude of play. And, this did seem like the kind of prank he might pull, just for laughs. But, if he was controlling this crowd for

THE CHURCH OF ARNOLD

fun, it was wrong, so wrong. By putting these people under his power, he turned them into dead people.

Clearly hearing my thoughts, Arnold started gesticulating wildly, though in a subdued way (since we were in church), that he had nothing to do with this Tuesday night event. I had often wondered what it would be like to spend a couple of hours inside of Arnold's head, in that learned mind-space. But, now I just wanted to get in there to know if he was lying - if he was a monster or innocent. But, at this point, I couldn't read his thoughts, as I was obsessed with my own panic.

Not knowing what else to do, I decided to listen to a bit of the preacher's sermon.

The preacher chimed, "Every anniversary of Arnold's speaking here, we have the annual tenet summary wherein we rehearse and remember our beliefs – Arnold's beliefs and the reasons for them." He spoke as if he were speaking to neighbors. This was a very friendly and local meeting.

"And, the inconvenient fact that this is a Tuesday evening, doesn't change our schedule at all." Slight laughter acknowledged the difficulty of arriving on a Tuesday night. "But, I want you to know that I appreciate your coming on a Tuesday night even more than I usually do." Arnold's haughty look indicated that the preacher's explanation cleared him of my suspicion.

"Yeah," I thought, "that or the preacher's responding directly to my fears means Arnold's even controlling the preacher moment-to-moment, his every word. He made him say that to shut me up! Even the light laughter could have been made to trick me into thinking he doesn't control them."

"And, so," the preacher continued, "our congregation renews the tenets of our beliefs, beliefs we find very, very important; beliefs we intend to spread with all the might that our little community has."

He paused as he surveyed his 'little community,' "Now, Mr. Arnold wrote that he lived between one 'dying world and another, powerless to be born.' That is, he lived in an age when religion was dying and the modern world hadn't quite come into being. People had stopped believing in Christianity and nothing had yet risen to replace it.

"And, this created a horrible vacuum. Christianity, the very essence of western civilization, was gone. And, we can, of course, still see the effects of what Arnold noted everywhere today. Our culture has a general lack of morality. Religion used to fight against hedonism. Religion provided us what Arnold called, 'Hebraism,' the moral power to do right, to follow laws, to answer to moral codes more elevated than our own individual whims.

"The Hebraic characteristic of religion told us that hard work is morally superior to doing drugs and shopping." This claim elicited a bit of laughter from the audience, as if they'd heard him preach on those sins before and remembered it well. But, as he uttered these words, an image of my mother dying in Dr. Les' apartment flashed into my mind. I shuddered a terrible black shudder. Yes, hard work beats drugs.

"But now," The preacher said pointedly, "our congregation seems to be among the only secular groups who remember such truths. That's why we need to get Arnold's secular Biblical vision out to the secular world.

"Science has shown that we can no longer take the Bible literally. And if religious folks keep on insisting that God is a real person in the sky, no modern person will listen to them. We believers in the Bible as a moral compass have to face these facts, my friends. There is no God in the sense of a man up in the sky as the mainstream Christians believe. Am I right?"

"Yes Sir," The crowd replied in unison.

"Arnold is definitely controlling this crowd." I thought. "No preacher would say that God isn't real. And, the crowd, not saying, 'Amen,' but saying 'Yes, Sir,' in unison, confirmed my fear. They are all speaking strangely as one. This is not normal. This whole Tuesday night sermon is a terrifying zombie show put on by the demon master himself, Mr. Arnold."

I decided to leave. But, Arnold looked like a clown as he shrugged and grimaced as if to ask 'What-did-I do?' When his smile went completely upside down in protest, I wanted to laugh, (though against my will). In nervous exhaustion, I just exhaled and stayed put.

Could this scenario be actually happening naturally? Could it be coincidence that we were here on the anniversary of Arnold's visit to this church? Was this a dream? I pinched myself, but didn't wake up. Arnold smiled normally, crossed his legs and leaned back to listen, as if the matter were settled.

After a full pause, the preacher continued. "Now, science tells us that if there is an effect there must be a cause.

Now I see people going to church all the time. This movement of people is an effect for which there must be a cause. And, if you want to know the cause ask the folks goin' to church, they'll tell you; They go to church because of God. So, we can scientifically prove that God has an impact in this world. Yes he does. No one can deny that!"

"Yes, Sir. Yes, Sir." They affirmed.
"Christianity is true because, we see the effects of it. We see people going to church weekly – and sometimes on Tuesdays!" The crowd laughed. "I don't necessarily believe Christ went into the sky, but I sure do believe in Christianity. Yes Sir I do. Christianity exists. No secular person can argue with that! It exists and has an effect in the world. We are all here because of Christ and His message."

"Yes, Sir. Yes, Sir." The crowd echoed in waves.

"We may not be supernaturalists - I see a few practicing and retired science teachers in the room - but, we can all say that Christianity and God exist in this world, in their effects. Yes, we can!"

"Yes, Sir. Yes, Sir." The attendants tapped their pews and made a terrible noise.

That made sense to me. And, as I found I was learning, as Arnold had promised, my mind started to wander from my obsession over whether or not he controlled the crowd, to the topic at hand.

"And, we need to spread the shocking truth, that a church, a real church, an active church, a loud show-up-on-Tuesday-night church, accepts both Christianity and secularism!"

"Yes, Sir. Yes, yes." The crowd murmured, gaining enthusiasm.

"And, here is where the central tenet of Arnoldian Christianity comes into play – rather than focus on the supernatural, on the Bible's claimed miracles - we have to plumb the meaning of the Bible – to look at it as literature.

"We cannot get people into church by expecting them to forget science and suspend reason. We have got to engage their reason, get them to engage in literary criticism, Bible-based literary criticism. We have to get them to appreciate the meaning of the Bible and its role in our culture. This is what Jesus would have wanted."

"Yes." The audience agreed – more mutedly now.

"With these Arnoldian precepts we get joy and rationalism, a beautiful way to understand the poetry of the soul, without losing our intelligence. For it is true, as we read in Proverbs, chapter twelve, verse one, that "Whoso loveth instruction loveth knowledge: but he that hateth reproof is brutish."

"Moves the heart and mind, don't it?" He asked the spellbound crowd.

"With Arnoldian Christianity, we get both spiritual enlightenment and a connection with our ancestors, our western biblical forefathers."

"And, we need to remember that Jesus is not only our moral savior, but the bedrock of our wonderful western civilization! It was Christ's valuing the individual and their soul, no matter how lowly, prostitute or not, that paved the way for democracy – the idea that every person's voice counts. This paved the way for rights and the freedom of speech.

"In this way, Jesus made us from nothing. Risen up just like Lazarus. Risen up, life from nothing! To praise Jesus is to praise the West, to celebrate all our rights, our freedom to self-cultivate."

Not hearing much, he prompted the audience, "Am I speaking truth brothers and sisters, historically verified truth?"

"Yes, Sir." The crowd said politely, prompting his call for affirmation,

"I asked, 'are you with me?'"

"Yes, Sir. Yes, Sir." The crowd yelped in affirmation, stamping their feet, and hitting the pews.

"Are you with me?" He repeated with more gusto and raising his hands.

"Yes, Sir. Yes, Sir!" The crowd swooned, adding screams to their banging. I even found enthusiasm boiling up in me. I had only once been to church before, with my childhood friend Amanda – and it bored me. But, this service moved me. It was a strange experience. I felt like something in me was going to burst.

After what seemed an eternity, the preacher relaxed back into a normal speaking voice, his shoulders relaxing as his hands stayed on the podium's corners, "This Sunday we will begin our annual reading of Arnold's beautiful book, *Literature and Dogma*.

THE CHURCH OF ARNOLD

"But, as we venture forth into reading it, I want you to understand that your reading the Bible, your communion with this church, is not just for you. No, Sir. It provides a road to salvation for our entire beloved nation.

"For Jesus told us, in John, chapter three, verse sixteen, 'God so loved the World that he gave his only Son, that whoever believes in him should not perish but have eternal life.' And if we cling to Jesus and the Bible, our nation can continue to live, to have eternal life."

"And, yes, ladies and gentlemen, when I speak of uplifting the nation, I am speaking of some heavy lifting." For as it warns in Revelation, chapter twenty-one, verse eight, "the fearful, and unbelieving, and the abominable, and murderers, and whoremongers, and sorcerers, and idolaters, and all liars, shall have their part in the lake which burneth with fire and brimstone: which is the second death."

This prompted spontaneous murmurs of agreement and sporadic 'Yes, Sirs.'

"And no," he calmed down and chuckled, "I don't literally think there is a lake of fire somewhere. But there will be national hell to pay if we don't clean up our act. Our decline can get worse. Our nation can collapse. And, that'll make the horrific hellfire imagery feel understated." To this the audience chuckled nervously in agreement.

"And, while the Revelations passage shows our potential doom in penetrating language, it also shows us the keys to our salvation: having respect, not desecrating our sacred national symbols, and knowing right from wrong. These are the biblical keys to our redemption. And, that's the vital literal truth, the literary truth that the Bible, the greatest piece of literature ever written by man, teaches us."

"So with this eventuality in mind, and love of life in our souls, let's rededicate ourselves to getting the message out of Arnoldian Christianity out into the world."

"Will we?" He asked three times in a row. Each time evoking a stronger cry of 'Yes, Sir!'
"Well then let's now rise and sing the song on page forty-two of our hymn book."

Rising with the other parishioners and finding page forty-two, Arnold and I sang with the congregation:

"Does God exist? Did Christ rise?
These we cannot know.
But he did go on that cross for us,
As such he loves us so."

"Noah's flood, Egypt's blood
In these we can't believe.
But we feel God's ever warm presence
Each and every Christmas Eve.

"Arnold, Arnold
Taught us the Bible new.
And so we rejoice in its words,
And we know it's true."

"Arnold, Arnold
Taught us the Bible new.
And so we rejoice in its words,
And we know it's true."

"Jonah's Whale, Noah's Ark,
It's the finest Art
These stories carried our nation high.
So we praise them in our heart.

"Arnold, Arnold
Taught us the Bible new.
And so we rejoice in its words,
And we know it's true."

The song over, the preacher started in on some announcements. Marguerite's confusion, the window of thought this service opened up for her; her – if you will – conversion; took her mind off her suspicions concerning me. As such, I once again took control of my thoughts.

I partially understood Marguerite's confusion. I understood that it seemed unlikely, beyond coincidence, that we just happened to show up on the anniversary of my visit to this little church. But, I resented her suspicion of me. I earned this little congregation with years of academic toil; with my three books on the Bible. And, after all of my guidance, she should have trusted me. Still, being the adult in the relationship, I provided her with a reassuring explanation.

"Thank you so very much, Dearest Dearheart, for having come to this event. I have long heard of it from the nether regions up above. I always look forward to reading the church's monthly 'Arnoldian Bible Studies' newsletter. And, I have long dreamed of visiting, here. But, alas, . . . "

At that a blood-curdling scream rang out and people ran away, scrambling from the pews and knocking chairs over, till they assembled around us in a semi-circle. A thick woman stood frozen with one hand over her mouth and another pointing at me. They could see me!

"Em, relax everybody, um . . ." I stammered nervously wiping the sides of my coat.

"Everyone, there is no need to worry," Marguerite jumped in. "He is a Matthew Arnold impersonator. We're doing a TV show about him."

"I saw him appear from nowhere!" The pointing woman said, still shaking and pointing.

"Well," I offered with both nerves and sincerity, "if I were Matthew Arnold's ghost, I could do nothing but applaud your efforts. This church, your dedication to our dear Mr. Arnold's magnificent message, your eloquent preacher, your wonderful singing voices, . . ."

"But, I saw her sitting by herself and I didn't see him enter at all!" An assertive man insisted.

"My dear Sir," I countered, "you, an Arnoldian! Of all people, couldn't really believe in ghosts."

"I don't know what I believe, but . . ."

"We'll definitely be making a documentary about you all, for the History Channel." Marguerite offered urgently as she tugged on my sleeve. "But, we really must roll along now. Thank you!"

People did not know what to do as we abruptly turned to take our leave. Then I made my fatal error, I walked straight through one of the pews.

At this a riot exploded. Many items got knocked over and the church doors banged as people flew out of them. I could hear cars starting and tires screeching outside as we ran outside to our own car with fright equal to anybody's. Marguerite hurriedly opened her door and jumped in the driver's seat. I, in my panic, just jumped through my door.

In all the confusion, for a couple of miles, Marguerite breathed hard and I fidgeted silently from nerves. Calmer, about ten minutes down the road, Marguerite remembered doubting me and felt badly about it. We looked at each other shrugged and sighed.

"This only happened once before," I reminisced. It was during the premiere of the 1940 version of the film, 'Tom Brown's School Days,' in London. My accidental appearance was in all of the newspapers. But people just wrote it off as a publicity stunt. I dare say it added to the film's success."

"I don't know how they'll explain this one." Marguerite added. "Imagine people dedicated to religion, with all the supernatural parts removed, seeing a ghost."

"My church is ruined." I said with real sadness.

"Well, I'll still believe." Marguerite offered meekly, guiltily.

"You'd better, or I'll come down and control people and get them to eat your brains! Brah ha ha!" At this we both laughed and she took her first normal breaths since the wide parishioner lady screamed.

CHAPTER
~ 19 ~

FAILURE

On the way back to Los Angeles, I told Marguerite more about my travels across America.

"The tour started with President Grant saying that the British lion – that's me – didn't roar loud enough!"

"What?"

"He couldn't hear me." I said, adjusting my volume.

"What?" She asked again.

Switching from speaking out loud to psychic communication, I tried to explain, "The auditoriums were very large and, . . ." Marguerite was nearly laughing, "Oh! Very funny."

"But, it was a real problem!" I protested, "I took speech lessons. But, people said they still couldn't hear me. And, when I said one bad thing about President Grant's grammar, Mark Twain started attacking me ruthlessly. Everywhere I went the papers railed against me as a snobby prig who didn't appreciate the practical mindset of Americans."

"So your trips to America were kind of a failure?" Marguerite asked.

"Oh no Dear, they were a huge gushing success!"

"Really?" She prodded, quizzically, wondering if there would be a punch line.

"I made more money than I expected!" Marguerite rolled her eyes and smirked. "Oh no Dear, this was serious. I was broke. After thirty-five years of inspecting schools, I could barely afford to retire. And, whereas I got no royalties from my book sales in America, (thanks to your lack of copyright law enforcement), my books made me well enough known that I was able to make money with this lecture tour."

"Well, I am glad you got money. But, did the people like your lectures?"

"How many people like something is not a good measure of its worth. I told Americans what they did not want to hear, Love. And, that was unpopular. Rather than deal with my arguments, they ridiculed me. I did not fail in America. I made my stand without compromise. America failed."

I said this rather defensively, but looking out at America, thinking about young Marguerite's life, I guess I did fail in America. My words had done nothing to forestall the degeneration of America or Americans. KFC uber alles.
And, honestly, I sensed the failure of my cause during my lifetime. In my youth I cultivated a romantic vision of individual poetic salvation. But, as with my overblown Empedocles, I found this anti-social, loner-vision hollow. And, so I married and moved on.

After my romantic vision failed, I turned to my doomed social-uplift-through literary criticism idea. If critics helped the public understand the difference between fluff and profundity, artists would produce better work. This would inspire all of us to search of our best selves. It was at this time that I considered the artist-as-religious figure vision.

Also at this time, I launched the field of Celtic studies. I naively thought that if I could contrast the sweetness and light of Celtic literature with England's stiff Puritanical Hebraic culture, I could shame England into cultural reform. What a fool. Celtic studies changing England!

When these plans didn't work, I suggested cultural guidance by the government, hoping that public schools might turn the middle class into cultural exemplars. The schools came into existence. But, with their 'payment for results' orientation, people just became more mechanized. Marguerite's sad 'education,' gave lie to that hope.

Disappointed, I tried to secularize religion. But this just stirred resentment. The religious community panned me as too secular. They said I was a 'culturist' not a 'theist' – that we needed real religion, not to just treat the Bible as literature, but as the true word of God.

And, they were correct. I really was a culturist. I really did see cultural standards as the road to social salvation – *the* way to guide society. But, though my culturist plans didn't work, neither did theirs. Religion was dying in my time. It hasn't saved England.

In my final decade I returned to doing pure literary criticism – analyzing the best thought and said - my favorite pastime. But, while this was great hedonistic indulgence for an old school inspector, it was also shadowed – if I am honest with myself – with a sense of failure. I kind of went full-circle and just retreated into my mind and the arts, as my suicidal romantic icon Empedocles had done, so many years before.

Oh, I didn't totally give up. I fought a bit. I went through the motions. I made my trips to America. I spoke of some small 'remnants' of elite thinkers saving civilization. But, perhaps the Americans were right to think me an out-of-touch, affected, old fool.

In total despair, I remembered my ultimate lines of self-doubt,

But who can say, without a fear:

That best, who ought to rule, am I;

The mob, who ought to obey, are these,

I the one righteous, they the many bad?

All totaled, during our drive back to Los Angeles, I felt more like a ghost than usual. The whole world had become, from my perspective a ghost town, a shell, with no 'ghost in the machine,' - as they say – all products, all material, no reverence for the human mind. But, I bitterly jibed, "There is no ghost in this machine, except me," And, I was nothing but a ghost; a real dead ghost.

While driving I often simply marveled at nature. That might have had something with the beauty of Utah's Bryce Canyon and the other wonders through which we drove. I didn't see evidence of civilization revitalized. But I had simpler sources of amazement, planet earth and my being on it again. These moments were overwhelming, even frightening in their beauty; sublime.

Upon first meeting Marguerite, I had no idea that I'd be permitted to stay with her for such a length of time. For part of our drive home, I got whisked back to the desert, finding the notes I had taken in the passenger seat neatly organized. I cried as I chronicled the beauty of our adventures. Because, while writing it, I had a sense that I would soon return to the nothingness of half-remembered pure intellect. My journey was coming to a close.

Near Los Angeles, the final mission prior to my departure became obvious as Marguerite began to fret over deciding what subject she'd study in university. She worried out loud about what her father would think. I knew that this was the last hurdle I was to help my oh-so-young charge with before departing.

"Daddy wants me to study something practical such as nursing, finance, or engineering." She hadn't even remembered to call her father, 'Father.' I was a failure.

"What do you expect, he's an American." I languidly replied.

'I'm an American!' Marguerite barked. But, then she gave me a nostalgic smile. I heard her remember how nastily and nationalistically Americans reacted to my message of cultural uplift, and she censored herself. Touchingly, she was ashamed that Americans, her people, had proven themselves to be philistines by being so angry at the suggestion that they cultivate themselves.

Marguerite had psychically heard me rehearsing my history of social uplift efforts. But, because she was preoccupied with deciding what her major should be, she missed my sense of despair. "To be effective at social reform," she thought, "studying European literature and 'the best that has been thought and said' is necessary." That was the first time I'd heard Marguerite consider undertaking such a mission.

As I heard her consider this tact, I couldn't help but feel its futility. But, even if hopeless, such a mission would have its moments of intrinsic beauty. Instinctively, psychically, I told her to remember 'sweetness and light' if she were to undertake such a campaign.

She looked at me and smiled.

"And Marguerite, I must say that I understand your father's position better than you might."

"Because you had a shi – sorry, a miserable job that you hated for so much of your life?"

"Exactly. Despite a reputation as a poet and scholar, exulted enough that I was made the Oxford Professor of Poetry, I could find no work with my degree that paid well. I had to endure thirty-five years of hard, promotion-free, boring labor. Whereas, in my day, businessmen, engineers and others associated with industry, retired young and wealthy."

"You didn't get promoted even once during your career?"

"No. And, here I'll admit, I was partially to blame. I was a pain-in-the-arse." We smiled at my informality. "I publically fought my education supervisors' mechanical pay-for-results program. I considered the idea of cramming basic rote facts into student's heads gross, not a way to cultivate a love of the mind or perfection. I paid dearly for my very public fight against my supervisors."

My depression was beginning to impact my young charge. "Then maybe I should get a practical major so I can support my art later." She said despondently.

"It never happens that way. My poem 'Summer Night' speaks to this:

"For most men in a brazen prison live,

Where, in the sun's hot eye,

With heads bent o'er their toil, they languidly

Their lives to some unmeaning task-work give,

Dreaming of naught beyond their prison-wall"

"And the rest, a few,

Escape their prison, and depart

On the wide ocean of life anew."

"Is there no life, but these alone?

Madman or slave, must man be one?"

"So I either become a madman or a slave?" She pleaded.

"No. You'll be a slave either way!" I smiled sadly.

"Oh this is just awful." She thought in a muddle.

"You must work. You have no choice to but to be a part of this world. But, just the same, you shouldn't wish to withdraw from this world. Though difficult, it is a fair world and a beautiful world. And, the world itself needs our attention to it.

"But, you must guide the world towards something. And that thing is perfection. Unfortunately, the idea of perfection as an inward condition of the mind and spirit is at variance with the mechanical and material civilization and its vacuous ideal of progress. To succeed you must have ideals, visions of perfection; you must be a beautiful madman as well as a slave.

"Drudgery is not the worst thing to fear." I continued laconically, "That is why, though I understand your father's concerns, they do not mean so much to me. For people like us, to our souls, having no ideas and money is worse than the reverse." At least that is the thought I comforted myself with.

I checked to find her following (what to study being on her mind). So I continued earnestly, "University will offer you the space to start this journey; a place where you can have free play of the mind, removed from society's pressures. University will give you roots that will feed you forever. Without it, you'll never see far beyond your walls. You'll work towards nothing, you'll be a mental slave."

Then she turned inward to her thoughts and stared at her hands on the steering wheel. I had given her too much to think about, on top of her pressing questions.

"Marguerite, you've seen me scribbling notes in the front seat during our commute, eh?"

"Yep."

"Well, that is how I had to write *Culture and Anarchy*, my religious works, and my writing on Celtic literature. I was not qualified for any work that paid well. But, none of these intellectual adventures would have happened without my university education. And, ultimately, my study of culture even framed and gave meaning to my school inspection work."

"Celtic literature! I'd love to talk about that!" She exclaimed, momentarily emerging from her immediate concerns.

"I'm afraid, My Sweet Dearest Marguerite, we haven't much time. But, when you go to university, and study European literature, you'll be able to find my books in the library and study them to your heart's content. But do appreciate it, because after university, time will be very short."

Then I looked at her so earnestly that she knew to turn her head in order to make full eye contact with me. "Dearest, may I be brutally honest?"

"Yes, please."

"Your schooling thus far has left you almost entirely illiterate in the literature of your mother tongue, let alone those of the continent, and the Greeks." As she took this to heart, I provided the remedy, "The good news is that you're young and you have time. But, don't only read what the teachers give you. Read all of the classics; become as great friends with Plato and Sophocles as you have become with me."

"Okay."

"And have fun. Always! Explore. Ignore all of my advice, but do fall in love with what you read."
"Okay. I'll ignore all your advice except about being in love with what I read - and that bit about one-fifth of life being dairy." We smiled at each other tenderly.

"Yes, dairy and pillows, depending on the hour of the day." I smiled, "Dairy and pillows."

CHAPTER

~ 20 ~

HOME AGAIN

Back in Los Angeles, Marguerite confessed to her father that she had, in fact, violated his orders and gone to see his ex-wife. She also told him of his ex-wife's death. Jack was only momentarily angry at Marguerite for having broken her promise and visited Cindy Rose, her adopted mother. He flushed out some half-felt, rehearsed indignation over her having lied. He knew she'd go there. For the most part, silence greeted the announcement.

We came to realize, however, that Marguerite's little rebellion had been good for her father. In fact, it proved healing for the whole family.

In the days that followed, it seemed a huge burden had been lifted from Jack's shoulders. At some level, he had still felt responsible for his ex-wife's life. He felt he had failed her; he felt himself a failure. But, both Jack and Marguerite now understood the depths of Cindy's personal problems. They didn't cause them.

As the self-blame and guilt dissolved, Jack came to trust that he was competent to take care of himself. This new confidence allowed him to exert himself more. He breathed with a new openness and stood more erect than he previously had. His soul was in more direct contact with his eyes, if that makes sense.

As a part of this transformation, Jack became less dominated by his girlfriend, Samantha. She, in turn, unconsciously appreciated not having to make all decisions alone. She felt much more secure in their relationship and much less of a need to quickly 'get hers' by manipulation. She trusted him. Theirs bloomed into quite a magical relationship.

Jack's newfound self-respect and Marguerite's new trust in him did wonders for their relationship as well. He felt competent – and so, in control. This meant that he no longer had to hold the reigns so tightly, to prevent her from injury due to his lackluster leadership and inability to protect her. He trusted himself, and so he could trust that Marguerite would be, with his guidance, safe.

As such, upon Marguerite's announcing her decision to study English literature, he only repeated a few lingering cautionary statements about poverty. And then he told her, "You're in Los Angeles, the land of film. With my connections, we'll think of something for you to do with that degree." Samantha looked on and nodded, assured by Jack's confidence.

At his acceptance of her study plans, Marguerite hugged both her father and Samantha individually. She appreciated the support each of them provided. And, at this sight, tears welled up in my eyes. I loved the new emotionality of my post-life, life. This was amongst the sweetest moments I had ever witnessed.

Back in her room, I had what I took to be my final words with Marguerite.

"Marguerite, I feel as if these will be the last words I will ever share with you. I know it. Our journey is closing and a new beginning awaits you."

"Mr. Arnold," Marguerite, sitting on the edge of her bed, started crying and put her head forward towards her knees, "I'll always remember you and I'll always love you." She too intuited that our sojourn was approaching its conclusion.

"Before I go, I want you to know a few things, the state of university 'liberal arts' departments being what they are," (I said with air-quotes over 'liberal arts'), "I wouldn't have recommended such a major to just anybody. I am recommending such a path to you, Dearest Blossom, because you are aware that you have a life of the mind."

She was completely slouched; as bent as when I had first met her. And, powerless to touch her chin, I waited for her head to come up so that I could lock onto her eyes. "Did you hear me?"

She nodded slightly in affirmation.

"Do you know what I mean by 'life of the mind'?" I prodded.

She again nodded, nearly invisibly, under her hair.

"Touch your head once if the answer is 'Yes.'"

She laughed and hit her head hard enough that she followed the blow with an audible, "Oww."

"Oh, you can make sound!" I exclaimed. She confirmed this by hitting herself on the head again! We both laughed very heartily this time. A few waiting tears were jarred loose and rolled down her cheeks.

I knew the moralistic theme of the commencement speech I was preparing to give, by heart. I recognized it as a variation of the sort of moralizing speeches my father used to make at his Rugby school - and at home.

But, now, looking back at my life, its failures, I had to second-guess the speech. Was it true? Should I tell my young charge to dedicate herself to the improvement of society? Would I send myself down the same path again?

My reforms had largely been failures. America, as our journey revealed, certainly was no better off for my existence. I despaired of hope that my beloved England was much better.

I could use my love of cultivating the sacred aspect of ourselves, our minds, to muster the resolve I needed to give a well-rehearsed self-cultivation speech. In the light of my failures though, pure literature seemed hedonistic, surrounded by despair, nearly nihilistic.

In a sense, I wanted to convert her from the romantic early period of my life to the more mature maaaarried concerns of my life. This had been a problem all along. I wished this young girl to be further advanced than she was. And perhaps, for the time being, she would be wiser to purely study humanities for the intrinsic uplift, even if it makes her an anti-social self-absorbed Romantic. Perhaps she would be better off if she lived her life rather than repeating my failures. Perhaps, I should just say goodbye and leave her be.

In the final moment, I thought of my pedantic father. He had saved the Rugby school and so, by creating administrators of the Empire, influenced the world. And, even if that mission proved vainglorious, in the long-run, Father had indelibly impacted his students and me, his son. If nothing else, Marguerite's public spiritedness and cultivation would help her offspring.

Though not clear of doubts, in my father's honor, I proceeded apace, (likely, I realized, for the last time), "Perhaps this is asking a bit much Marguerite, but I'd have you remember to not only study for yourself - to be your best self - but to uplift society; Be more than just a hedonist, be a culturist.

"Seek social perfection as you seek your own. I think, because of your own personal history - and our time together - the connection between the general culture and personal cultivation, will be clearer to you than to most."

"It's clear to me. All of it is. Especially because of having spent this time with you. If you hadn't been with me Mr. Arnold, . . . " Marguerite veered towards dramatic tears.

"Dearest, My Heart, I'm not done with my speech yet." I preemptively cut her off with a smile.

"Sorry." Marguerite smiled and bowed with her head, holding back the emotional tornado with composure and conduct.

"And so, to be clear, if I had one wish for you, Marguerite, I'd wish that you'd write. Writing is the key to the life of the mind. To write is to be enlightened, to knowing – to exploring - what you yourself actually know and think.

"And, again, don't just write for yourself, but write publically. Publish. Write as though civilization depended upon it. Human progress consists in a continual increase of the number of those who, (ceasing to live by the animal life alone, by the senses alone), come to participate in the life of the mind. Make this increase your goal.

And, I, sensing that I'd let things get too heavy, even for this auspicious and poignant moment, added, "And, always write with a sense of fun!" I emphasized this with a little awkward pose. "Engaging the philistines is a wonderful sport. And, if you ever drop the sweetness and light, you'll become just another nasty crank. Remember that when you write. Have fun."

She started to say something and I interrupted her one last time, "Epp, I'm not done young lady."

She bowed, made little seated half-curtsy and mumbled, "My Lord."

"And, above all Dear, my dear young Marguerite, please have a big family! Apart from my time with you, and writing, my happiest times were with My Essential Incomparable Lovely Flu and our family." I paused for a effect, "But, wait a couple of years on that one!"

She raised her eyebrows to ask, and I confirmed, "That's it."

"Mr. Arnold, I can't tell you how much, . . ."

"Don't attempt to." I cut her off. "Sometimes words are wholly inadequate. We both know what we mean to each other."

As she nodded, I began to rise and fade. My body and ideas faded until all that was left was sadness at seeing my dear, dearest, sweet, Marguerite crying below.

EPILOGUE

I returned to a scream that nearly gave me second fatal heart attack. And, to make matters worse, after screaming, Marguerite ran to hug me. Predictably, she tripped on the coffee table behind me, injuring her shin, went over the table, and landed between the table and the sofa. And then she let out another type of scream.

At that, her husband, rushed into the room. And, seeing her lying down crying and me standing facing her, he ran and jumped on my back with similar painful results. Crawling the rest of the way off the table, to be next to his wife, he looked back at me. And seeing my face, the young man now fearfully let out a scream that was at least as loud as Marguerite's first welcoming scream. I had made quite an entrance.

"Anthony, Darling, Anthony," Marguerite pleaded, gently drawing his thin gasping head, towards her, and away from me, as his arm continued pointing in horror, "it's Matthew Arnold, he's a ghost, he's my friend, it's okay." So tender to be remembered as a friend, my eyes started to moisten.

"Look," she pointed at my emotional state, "He's a regular mushball. There is no need to be frightened or defend me. Say 'Hello, Mr. Arnold.'"

I raised my hands high, took what felt like a breath, scrunched my face like that of a lion and roared as loudly as I could. Marguerite's man nearly recoiled under the sofa. But, I couldn't keep in character. I burst out laughing. "I'm so sorry my dear man, I couldn't resist the joke! I'm so sorry. I am, as dearest Marguerite said, Matthew Arnold, . . . and harmless - aside from my unforgivable sense of humor."

Then, turning in the direction of Marguerite's gaze, I saw the most beautiful sight: A child, a boy, about eight years old, with reddish dirty blond hair cut to his shoulders. It was Marguerite's boy. I began to shake with joy and get emotional again. For his part, the child's young eyes darted back and forth between his parents and me in mute silence.

"Matthew, come here." Marguerite ordered. Matthew! This was my little namesake! I vaguely remembered having seen his name in the acknowledgements of one of Marguerite's books.

The boy ran across the room and into the arms of his mother and father. Like a pieta with child, the mother comforted the trio. "Matt, Mother and Father are alright. We are safe. This is Mother's friend, Matthew Arnold. He has the same name as you!" She said this with an intense smile and direct look into my eyes. You can imagine my elation.

A tell tale sign of a wonderful family life, the boy, (if not the father), felt perfectly safe at her reassurance. The effect came from the happy calm in her voice.

"My Dear Marguerite, - and Anthony is it? – you're hurt. Are you alright?" I smiled, held my waist and tilted forward a bit to indicate care.

"My shin is a bit torn," Marguerite reported, with some obvious pain cutting into the joy and comedy of this moment. "Anthony Honey, are you okay?"

"I am in a state of shock; and not a mild one!" He replied.

"Good, then you're normal." Marguerite quipped, smiling at me, "Let's unwind." And as they did, I took a deep breath and drank in this vision of the three of them disentangling themselves, and sitting up straight between the coffee table and the couch.

"Matt, do you see that man?"

"Yes," the boy said attentively with his eyes on me, "You're named after him. He is a very important friend to this family. And, I want you to be very polite to him."

"So, very, very happy to meet you Young Matthew." I replied, grinning broadly, without any pretense.

"Matthew." Marguerite said with a little sternness, "Conduct!"

"Pleased to meet you too, Sir." The little man responded, standing up.

"Mr. Arnold," Marguerite insisted.

"Mr. Arnold, Sir, glad to meet you." The boy dutifully corrected himself.

As he held out his little hand, Marguerite understood my nervousness about shaking it; my hand would go through his. Resourcefully, she patted young Matthew on the buttocks, "Now go get Flu and K."

At that command my heart fluttered up another level. She looked up at me and smiled even brighter, and I completely burst into tears that turned into embarrassed laughter, before returning to more controlled happy conduct again.

"Come on, go." The young mother said, with a firmer swat on the buttocks.

As little Matthew scurried away, Marguerite turned to her husband and said, "Now My Dear Darling Anthony, now do you believe me that Matthew Arnold accompanied me on a road trip in my youth?"

The shock still trimmed his ability to speak. To ease him out of his shock, with some feigned irritation she warned, "Anthony, Dearest, don't you be rude. Don't make me swat you on the butt too. Say hello to our guest."

"Well, okay then, alright, hello Mr. Arnold," Anthony uttered as he stretched out his hand to shake mine, "I am pleased to meet you in person at long last."

"And, I am overjoyed to make your acquaintance." I started, "Only don't bother with the handshake. As you might have noticed, . . ." and I put my right arm through my left arm to finish the point.

At that, young Matthew returned with his little sisters in tow. Silently, sleepily, having been woken by the noise, if not their brother, and amazed by my visage, the two little angels peered out, frozen, from the doorway. At that, another huge load of tears burst through my face. I quickly swallowed them as to make an appropriate impression – things being what they were.

"Flu, K, don't be rude, say hello to Mr. Arnold." My heart soared again at hearing my wife and sister's names while looking at these precious new beings.

The pair looked at each other and in unison extended their little arms and mumbled, "Hello, Mr. Arnold."

I went down on my right knee and, hands at my side, replied, "Hello, My Little Darling Sweethearts." I looked over at Marguerite who was, at this point crying behind a big smile. Having followed my eyes and seeing their mother's emotion, the little girls ran over to their parents and hugged them. Little Matthew followed. What a sight. My Marguerite had a family. And, their names made me feel that I had a new family too.

Marguerite called her agent and Anthony called his school so that they might stay home for the day. He was nearly as tall as I am, quite thin, and sported a very heavily trimmed beard that went just ever-so-slightly beyond a five o'clock shadow. And he wore a somewhat too large white shirt and a black tie. After the kids went off to school, we spoke for hours.

There were misty eyes as I confirmed that I could, in fact, read, though blurrily, the articles and books Marguerite wrote. She said she always thought of me reading in heaven when writing; She put my name in her work excessively, with the hopes that doing so would get them to me. Anthony now came to understand why she had so resolutely insisted that the children have the names that they do.

This, perhaps thirty year old, mother's voice had an upbeat exuberance, a confidence bordering on haughtiness about it. Her voice had a touch of pride that reminded me of – well – me.

And, physically, she had grown into an adult woman. This fact might seem too obvious to mention. But in my suspended, near-senseless, consciousness, I felt that I had only been gone for a couple of months. It took a long time for my mind to stop bouncing back and forth from the image I had of her at seventeen and the mother of three now before my eyes.

This was complicated by the fact that she wore a purple velvet sports jacket with a large gold broach on a flower-patterned shirt. This all much different than the long-sleeved t-shirt I was used to seeing young Marguerite in. Her green corduroy pants completed the ensemble, making her look as garish as – well, again – me.

Anthony got over my strange status relatively quickly. He seemed to be sturdy, upright fellow – very clean, very earnest. Like my Incomparable Lovely Essential Flu, he had an engaging, if not flamboyant, personality; his comically-too-large shirt and worn-for-duty tie fit him perfectly.

But I really came to fancy Anthony when I heard that he'd taken a middle school teaching position straight out of university to support my Marguerite while she went to graduate school.

And, Anthony's investment in Marguerite had paid off. She had become, to hear her tell it, quite the academic superstar. My young protégé taught at universities and had served as an editor on not one, but two journals concerning Victorian literature. She had, appropriately enough, become known as one of the world's leading

Arnold scholars (not that there were many to compete against).

"So Mags," Anthony joked, "this explains so much! I knew you were a wonderful mother and fantastic wife. But, now I know how you became such an expert on Mr. Arnold without hardly ever reading any of his books or poetry!"

They both smiled ever so broadly, so that I'd know this was a joke. And, Marguerite teased him back, "So glad you fiiinally believe me about what I've been trying to tell you about my days with Mr. Arnold."

"Yes. And, Honey, Mags, I am sorry for only laughing when you told me before. I really didn't know what to make of it. In fact, I've never really known how to compute your fantasy life about having spent the most important times of your life with a dead man. No offense." He said, glancing my way.

"None taken, I am sure." I responded. "It is understandable, isn't it Marguerite? After all, my existence is quite the miracle." And, at that, I posed as if hamming it up for a photograph – my right elbow parallel to my shoulder and my hand flared above my head.

As I had expected, Marguerite's father, Jack, had married Samantha. The now retired couple traveled quite a bit, but spent a lot of time with Marguerite, Anthony and the kids.

Marguerite reminded me, unnecessarily, how important my guidance concerning family life had been. When she had first read of my childhood, she couldn't imagine supportive, idyllic lives were really possible. But, with the ideal of my childhood in front of her, she knew what she wanted. Aside from Anthony, she considered Jack and Samantha her best friends. She couldn't be happier.

And, to my delight, Christina - Marguerite's half-sister whom we met when we visited her biological mother, Twinkie - had moved to Los Angeles and become Marguerite's assistant. We thought of calling Christina and inviting her over. But, we decided against it. She might lose her mind, we reasoned. Besides, Marguerite and Anthony decided that they'd enjoy jointly lording the secret over her in the years to come.

Looking back, we had reason to suspect a drive towards something finer in shy Christina. Her character, we retrospectively realized, was reminiscent of Marguerite's silent smirkiness. Marguerite told me how she and Anthony frequently stayed up late with Christina during *her* years in graduate school.

Even if I hadn't saved England or America, I had helped introduce two young people to the life of the mind. "The ape-man of evolution inclines towards Greek," I quipped, employing a line I often used in my fight with those who wished to replace the humanities in the school curriculum with science.

"And, so the soul also rises," Marguerite replied, showing off one of her many - I found out - popular clichés. Christina, Anthony, and other academics, it turned out, did not constitute the whole of Marguerite's intellectual community.

A friend of Marguerite's father, someone in the television business, found her airs and boldly stylish clothes charming. Very quickly, after getting her doctorate, she found herself called on to be a pundit – as public intellectuals are now called – on television.

With her visible eccentricities, flair for quotable material and sharp barbs, she had grown a formidable following amongst audiences of all ages. People, and not just comedians, imitated her voice and mannerisms. As many of her catchphrases reflected mine, I took some personal pride in her success.
"Show business," she told me, "is four-fifths conduct and one-fifth catchphrases."

"If you don't have any dairy," Anthony added – apparently having been let in on this inside joke.

"Or pillows," I added to warm, loving laughter.

In fact, Marguerite blatantly stole some of my catchphrases, such as 'sweetness and light.' In mock indignation, I raised the objection that I had stolen the formulation from Jonathan Swift before she was born, and – as the first person to steal it – the phrase should remain mine.

One of her catchphrases that I particularly liked was the idea of 'Heroic Reading.' And, in this vein, she had created the Matthew Arnold Scholarship to cultivate a generation of 'heroic readers,' a 'brigade of scholars,' of my work and related literature, (which included, she reassured me, Greek language, the Bible and European literature).

"That ought to keep you lingering for a while!" She poked at me.

'Yes, but was it good?' was another of her catchphrases. People frequently say a film is 'good' and just mean 'enjoyable.' Her reply turned peoples' attention to the fact that 'good' is also a moral evaluation; She'd quip, 'good meaning edifying, pro-social, and wholesome.' Such catchphrases got critics to start asking whether art made our 'souls rise' or 'portrayed us as beasts.'

'Watcha readin'?' was another that she used. At first it took her interviewers totally by surprise. But, then television personalities and everyday folk started asking each other this question, and reading steadily rose. She'd invariably use her interviewer's answers, as I would, to get into a light discussion on morality and the spiritual nature of our being.

Most of all, she told me, she was grateful to me for having taught her the value of charm. This allowed her to be confrontational without making people defensive. She always smiled broadly as she called people 'philistines.' And, her pose was making society – she sloganeered – 'less brutal and more intelligent.'

In fact, just the other day, she told me, the President of the United States spoke of Pericles and pontificated on the importance of masculine virtues to the survival of the Rome!

"Well!" I exclaimed, with a blend of humorous understatement and real pathos. "While my writing and dreaded lecture tours only shamed a few people into cultivation, it seems your engaging mass-media presence has had a real impact."

"No. It was always us." She kindly replied, "Oh, and," Marguerite then suddenly remembered excitedly, "in my early television appearances, I promoted Arnoldian Christianity. And, not only had the 'faith' grown," she said, with air-quotes around 'faith,' "but our little visit to their church had become cryptically legendary."

"It's 'We.' 'You and I.' 'We' have accomplished a lot." She then reached out to put her hand on mine. And, for once, I was not ephemeral. Her hand actually rested on mine. The moment was so sweet that my heart almost broke with joy.

"Well," I said in amazement, taking it all in, "I had always wondered why I was allowed to stay with you for so very long, my Dearest Heart. And, now I have my answer."

Of course, Marguerite needed me, just like the others. Without my interference, as so many others with her wretched pedigree, I sense she really might have died via suicide, at that overpass, at the age of seventeen. But, the powers-that-be must have sensed that western culture also needed a guide. And they knew that Marguerite had potential.

"That only solves one mystery, though," Anthony noted. As he had our attention, he finished the thought. "That might explain why you were allowed to stay so long with Mags in the past. But, it doesn't explain why you're back here now."

"Quite." I uttered with a renewed sense of dissatisfaction over not being able to solve this mystery.

"I know why you're here!" Marguerite exclaimed excitedly. And at that, she jumped up and left the room. In her absence, Anthony gave me a shrug. A minute later, she returned with a box. Upon opening it, she reached in and pulled out a bunch of loose papers and my notebook from our travels.

"My writing!" I exclaimed, "from our journey."

"Yes, I saved it. I always had a suspicion that you'd come back and finish this book."

And, through the next two weeks I had the enormous pleasure of writing the book that you, Dear Reader, are very close to finishing.

When I wasn't writing, I got to hold long discussions concerning science, art and politics with Anthony and Marguerite. Eventually, Christina even came over and joined in the debates (she really had developed her mind). And, as in life, I had an immensely wonderful time playing with the children, and the 'other animals,' in the nearby parks.

EPILOGUE

Upon finishing the prior paragraph, I wrote the following letter, left it on the finished manuscript, and bodily disappeared:

- - - - - - -

My Dearest Wonderful Marguerite,

Well, we finally know why I was allowed to remain with you so long. You are a smashing success and very important to the cultivation of America and, by extension, my beloved England, the West and the world.

And, now, as a small bonus, the powers-that-be allowed me to stay and finish the manuscript beneath this letter: our manuscript. I hope that you can use your celebrity to publish it. You needn't use my name as I am sure that professing a belief in ghosts would tarnish your stellar reputation.

It delights me no end to think that when people read this book, it will bring our friendship into my otherwise largely departed consciousness. In my long life, (now so much longer than I had anticipated), knowing you is absolutely one of the memories I cherish most.

Finally, your family's existence means the world to me. I feel giddy over my spiritual kinship with them. Thank you for creating a worthy cultural environment for them, My Darling Parental Guide. You're a gem on every level.

With love always,

Mr. A